Nationalism: A Religion

THE MACMILLAN COMPANY
NEW YORK • CHICAGO
DALLAS • ATLANTA • SAN FRANCISCO
LONDON • MANILA

IN CANADA
BRETT-MACMILLAN LTD.
GALT, ONTARIO

NATIONALISM:
A Religion

By
CARLTON J. H. HAYES
Seth Low Professor Emeritus of History in Columbia University

New York
THE MACMILLAN COMPANY   1960

The Macmillan Company, New York
Brett-Macmillan Ltd., Galt, Ontario

Printed in the United States of America

Library of Congress catalog card number: 60–13228

A Personal Apology

Most of my adult life has been devoted to observation and study of nationalism. My interest in it was first aroused by the outbreak of World War I. That event took me by surprise and shocked me out of the easy optimism about a future of uninterrupted progress and international peace which I had shared with many of my generation; and it showed me, too, that merely economic considerations did not really explain the ultra-patriotic popular acceptance of war. In the autumn of 1914 I wrote for the *Political Science Quarterly* a first article on nationalism.

Since then I have treated of nationalism in three books and part of a fourth;[1] in numerous articles, including an extensive one for the *Encyclopaedia of the Social Sciences*, and innumerable lectures; in graduate courses and seminars conducted for twenty-five years at Columbia University and occasionally for a semester or so at California (at Berkeley), Johns Hopkins, Western Reserve, Stanford, Michigan State, and Boston College; and, most important, in directing, and profiting from, many masters' essays and some sixty or seventy doctoral dissertations on various phases of the subject. I trust this apparent boasting will be forgiven a veteran who, in keeping now with the whole world, is still obsessed with nationalism.

The subject is indeed a very big one, with very many aspects. An exhaustive treatment, were it within any man's competence, would be exhausting. The present book makes no pretense of being exhaus-

[1] *Essays on Nationalism* (1926), *France a Nation of Patriots* (1930), *Historical Evolution of Modern Nationalism* (1931), and *A Generation of Materialism, 1878–1900* (1941), especially chs. VI, VII.

tive. It is simply a précis, a brief summing up, of what one person, through a lifetime of study, has conceived and learned about nationalism, with special regard to its story in Europe and with tentative reflections on its present course on other continents.

Many other and more detailed treatises about the general phenomenon have appeared during the past forty years, and it has been variously analyzed and discussed in terms of political science, literature, psychology, economics, sociology, statistics, even "intensity of communications." With a wide range of such studies I am familiar; to many I am indebted; from some I dissent. My own thinking and writing have been historical, and I think the broadly historical is the best and most helpful approach to an intelligent understanding of nationalism, cf how and why it has become the paramount preoccupation of the world today.

As becomes the historical art, the present book, it is hoped, is factually accurate and sanely interpretative, though it is without the scholarly apparatus which is the badge, and often the encumbrance, of "scientific history." There is no bibliography, and footnotes are sparse. The small number of references are mainly to writings of mine or of former students of mine; very occasionally, to some other and outstanding authority on the subject. Anyone desirous of more detailed study should consult Koppel S. Pinson's annotated *Bibliographical Introduction to Nationalism* (Columbia University Press, 1935), now somewhat out-of-date, but still basic and useful. Supplementary and fuller, though less critical, is Karl W. Deutsch's *Interdisciplinary Bibliography of Nationalism, 1935–1953* (Technology Press of M.I.T., 1956). There is also a valuable select bibliography appended to Boyd C. Shafer's interesting *Nationalism, Myth and Reality* (Harcourt, Brace, 1955).

A note of semantic caution! I regard language as a normal and fundamental part of the meaning of the words "nationality" and "nationalism," and it is difficult for me to understand why it is frequently denied or ignored. One reason, I suppose, is failure to recognize, on the one hand, the fundamental common nationality of Englishmen and English-speaking Americans, or that of Spaniards and Spanish-

Americans, and, on the other hand, the dual nationalities in Canada and Belgium or the triple in Switzerland. Another and related reason is ambiguity, with resulting confusion, in the use of the words "nation," "nationality," and "nationalism." "Nation," etymologically derived from the Latin term for "race" or "birth," originally had tribal significance but latterly has been loosely employed to denote not only a "people" or "folk" or "nationality" but any independent or sovereign state, such, for example as Switzerland or the Austrian or Russian Empire, whose polyglot citizens are referred to, quite perplexingly, as of Swiss or Austrian or Russian "nationality." In a similarly confusing way, vigorous assertiveness by a state, regardless of the kind of state, or by a group within it, has been called "nationalism." And particularly in France a curious distinction is drawn between *le patriotisme national* and *le nationalisme:* the one, as held by progressive "Leftists," is good; the other, confined to reactionary "Rightists," is bad.

Let me explain that in the following pages, as in earlier writings, I have let the loose word "nation" shift for itself and have not tried to moor it to any exact dictionary definition. But I have attempted to clear the words "nationality" and "nationalism" of ambiguity and of any moral or partisan connotation, and to attach to them the single, simple meanings set forth in the introductory chapter.

This book is history, not prophecy. When I am asked nowadays what I think will be the future of the world triumph—and world religion—of nationalism, I fall back on the concluding paragraph of an article which I wrote almost thirty years ago and which is truer now than then: "Nationalism is now obviously a world-wide phenomenon, vitally affecting both the material and the intellectual development of modern civilization. It tends more and more to influence the economic and spiritual as well as the political relationships of mankind. It is so closely related to the whole complex of contemporary culture that any future change in its direction or intensity would seem to wait upon an alteration of other factors in the complex."

CARLTON J. H. HAYES

July 18, 1960

Contents

Contents

CHAPTER I

What Nationalism Is

1. *Bases of Nationality: Language and Traditions*

Nationalism is an obvious and impelling movement in the modern and contemporary world. It is so obvious, indeed, and so frequently mentioned in the news, that it is apt to be taken for granted, like the rising and setting of the sun, and its importance overlooked.

Nationalism, as we know it, is a modern development. It has had its origin and rise in Europe, and through European influence and example it has been implanted in America and all other areas of Western civilization. But it is now no longer peculiar to the Christian West.

It has recently become an outstanding feature of states and peoples throughout the vast expanses of Asia and Africa, amid the traditional civilizations of Muslim, Hindu, Confucian, and Buddhist. It is especially evidenced across the whole breadth of the Muslim world: in the Turkey of Atatürk, in the Iran of Riza Pahlevi, in the Egypt of Nasser, in the separation of Pakistan from India, in the successful revolt of Indonesia against the Dutch, in the recently won independence of Libya, the Sudan, Somalia, Tunis, and Morocco, and in the Algerian rebellion. It is basic to the conflict between Arabs and Israelis.

Moreover, to a fully developed nationalism in Japan have now been added the nascent and militant nationalisms of India, Burma, Ceylon, Malaya, Vietnam, Cambodia, Laos, Thailand, and, most recently, of colored peoples almost everywhere in Africa. In its latest stage, nationalism is proving the dissolvent of oversea colonial empires of

1

Britain, France, the Netherlands, and Belgium, and probably too, before long, that of Portugal. And we should not overlook the fact that nationalism, as well as communism, is a mark of contemporary Russia and China.

What actually is this nationalism which is now so universal? It may best be understood, I think, by concentrating attention on Europe, and at first on western Europe. For here is its original home; here, its roots demonstrably reach far back into the past; and here, for at least five centuries, it has been an increasingly important factor in the evolution of our historic civilization.

In simplest terms, nationalism may be defined as a fusion of patriotism with a consciousness of nationality. For proper understanding of the matter, both *nationality* and *patriotism* require some explanation.

For centuries and for millenniums—as far back as we have any historical knowledge—the world has contained a large number of different nationalities. In Europe, the smallest of the five major continents, there has long been a variety of diverse nationalities: Greek, Latin, Celtic, German, Baltic, Slavic, Magyar, and so forth, some thirty-three at least at the present time.

Now what is a *nationality?* The word derives from the Latin *natio*, implying a common racial descent, but few, if any, modern nationalities consist of a distinctive "race" in the biological sense. Frenchmen are a nationality compounded of such different types as Mediterranean, Nordic, and Alpine. Germans include long-headed blonds and round-headed brunets. Italians represent curious mixtures of Etruscans, Phœnicians, and primitive Celts, of Saracens, Goths, and Norsemen. And in the United States Negroes belong, not to any African nationality, but, along with whites and red men, to the American nationality. Every nationality of which I have knowledge has been, or is, biologically and racially, a melting pot.

Nor is nationality determined simply by physical geography. To be sure, certain cultural features of Arctic peoples are bound to differ from those of tropical peoples, and both from life in temperate zones. For geographical reasons Czechs can hardly be expected to become a seafaring nationality, or the English not to become such. Yet, something other than geography has to explain why Englishmen from their island built up in modern times a great navy and merchant marine, while Irishmen from their adjacent island didn't. Or why similar habitats, climates, and pursuits failed to weld Frenchmen and Germans into a single nationality. Or why mountainous ruggedness of Scotland and Switzerland is supposed to explain the proverbial thriftiness of their inhabitants, but fails utterly to do so in the case of Dutchmen or of the French peasantry.

No, a nationality receives its impress, its character, its individuality, not, unless very incidentally, from physical geography or biological race, but rather from cultural and historical forces. First and foremost among these I would put *language*.

Language is peculiarly human, and at least ever since the legendary Tower of Babel there has been a wide, fluid, and baffling variety of languages. Anthropologists have shown that primitive tribes are marked off from one another by differences of speech. And alike to scholars and laymen it should be obvious that language is the surest badge of nationality. It is the one thing which all persons of a particular country have in common, whether they be rich or poor, good or bad, intelligent or stupid; and it is the one thing which distinguishes them from all other persons. It is common, for example, to all Germans, whether they be long-headed or round-headed, whether they live on the Alpine heights of the Tyrol or at sea level in Hamburg; and it differentiates them from all Frenchmen, including those who may be just like Germans in race and habitat.

Likewise, language is a tangible tie between the present generation of a nation and preceding generations. The English language ties the subjects of Elizabeth II with those of Elizabeth I, and Americans of the twentieth century with those of the seventeenth and eighteenth. Similarly the German language joins people who heard Martin Luther with those who have more recently listened to Adolf Hitler and now hear Konrad Adenauer. Of every nationality, language bespeaks both the solidarity and the continuity of a people. And national literature, in its many forms of prose and poetry, history, and romance, does much to emphasize what is supposedly peculiar to a nationality rather than what is fundamentally common to mankind.[1]

Along with language, and a close second to it in importance in constituting a nationality and distinguishing it from others, are *historical traditions*. These comprise an accumulation of remembered or imagined experiences of the past, an accumulation differing in content and emphasis from one linguistic group to another.

There are several kinds of historical tradition and background. There is (*a*) a people's religious past, whether, for instance, it was traditionally Christian, and if so whether Catholic like Italy or Spain, or Protestant like Sweden, or Eastern Orthodox like Greece or Russia, or divided between different forms of religion, like Germany and the United States. Religious traditions, it should be stressed, have been very important in shaping human culture, not merely by providing certain beliefs, but by establishing and maintaining particular social *mores*, observances, and habits, and by influencing literature and law.

There is also (*b*) a people's territorial past, its ancestral soil, involving a popular, sentimental regard for a homeland where one's forebears lived and are buried, a homeland that, though perhaps now fallen somewhat from a once high estate, still evokes memory and emulation of past greatness and glory. I need only mention, by way of illustration, the appeal of Jerusalem and Palestine to Jews, the "auld sod" to Irish, the Hellenic lands and isles to Greeks.

Then there is (*c*) a people's political past, whether their nation was detached from a big empire or expanded from a tribal state, whether it dominated other peoples or was long subject to alien rule, what government it has traditionally had—monarchical or republican, absolutist or constitutional, or democratic. There is (*d*) a people's fighting past, its exploits of valor and prowess, whether chiefly by land or by sea, whether victorious or vanquished. A people may be more united and nationalistic through grief over defeat than through

[1] I would hope that anyone who doubts the basic importance of language might read and ponder a volume recently published at Leiden in the Netherlands: H. L. Koppelmann's *Nation, Sprache und Nationalismus* (1956). There is also an arresting chapter on language in Rupert Emerson's *From Empire to Nation* (Harvard Univ. Press, 1960), pp. 132–148.

celebration of triumph. Serbs for centuries have recalled in glowing verse and fireside folk tales their valorous but disastrous defeat by the Turks at Kossovo in 1389. The epic fate of the "Invincible Armada" in 1588 stirred and spurred vanquished Spain scarcely less than victorious England.

There is, besides, (*e*) a people's industrial and economic past, whether it has been more or less advanced—"progressive" or "backward," to use a contemporary dichotomy—in agriculture, or trade, or manufacturing, or in all three, or has been famous for some specialized industry, and whether, too, it has had greater or less class wealth and distinctions. Lastly we may mention (*f*) a people's cultural past, what distinctive and distinguished literature and architecture and pictorial arts and music it has produced, and what scholarship and learning and degree of popular literacy.

2. *Fluidity and Complexity of Nationality*

All the foregoing and similar *historical traditions* are matters of culture, and so is *language*. Together, they constitute the cultural bases of nationality. Hence I would define nationality as "a cultural group of people who speak a common language (or closely related dialects) and who possess a community of historical traditions (religious, territorial, political, military, economic, artistic, and intellectual)." When such a group—such a nationality—cherishes in marked degree, and extols, its common language and traditions, the result is *cultural nationalism.*

Cultural nationalism may exist with or without political nationalism. For nationalities can and do exist for fairly long periods without political unity and independence. A notable example has been the Jewish or Israeli nationality; and scarcely less notable have been the Gaelic or Irish, the Polish, and the several Balkan nationalities. A nationality may be partitioned among two or more states, like the German or the Italian or the Basque, or it may be incorporated with others in a single state, like Switzerland or Belgium. Switzerland includes portions of three nationalities: German, French, and Italian. Belgium contains parts of two: French and Dutch-Flemish. If we are to grasp what a nationality is, we must avoid confusing it with state or nation. There is a Swiss state and nation, but, strictly speaking, no Swiss nationality. In like manner, there is a Belgian state and nation, but not a Belgian nationality.

The tendency has been, of course, for cultural nationalism to lead to political nationalism, and for each nationality to strive to establish an independent national state of its own. Yet, even in Europe, this goal has not yet been completely achieved. Countries which are usually thought of as possessing long-established national states, such as Great Britain, France, and Spain, still harbor national minorities with dissident languages and traditions. Besides Englishmen, Britain has Scots, Welsh, and some Irish. Besides Frenchmen, France has Provençals, Bretons, and Flemings. Besides Castilians, Spain has Catalans, Basques, and Portuguese-Galicians.

We should recognize, moreover, the fluidity of nationalities in the long run of history, and the existence of what may be called "sub-nationalities" or "secondary nationalities." Nationality has always existed throughout human history, just as there has always been differentiated human culture with variety of languages and customs and traditions. But specific nationalities have appeared and disappeared, risen and fallen. We know that in antiquity there were Hittite and Phœnician and Etruscan nationalities, Elamite and Edomite nationalities, but where are they now? They are gone, quite swallowed up long ago; only their names and some of their monuments remain. On the other hand, when they throve, where then were the French and English nationalities? These were nonexistent; their distinctive languages were not formed in antiquity, but only in the Middle Ages.

Since the sixteenth century, members of European nationalities have migrated overseas, carrying with them their languages and traditional culture. Thus the American continents were partitioned among Spanish, Portuguese, French, and English nationalities, and South Africa became the home of a segment of the Dutch nationality. All this developed when America and South Africa—to say nothing of Australasia and the Philippines—were far more remote from Europe than they are today. Then there were only sailing vessels and no cables or radio or airplanes. The remoteness of the oversea settlers from Europe and the novel frontier life they led, coping with strange lands and strange peoples, gradually served to qualify and add to the historical traditions which they had originally brought with them from the mother country.

Eventually, as we know, the widening differences were accentuated by the forceful revolutionary breaking of political ties, so that in the Americas an independent United States of English-speaking people emerged, and likewise a group of independent republics of Spanish-speaking peoples, an independent Portuguese-speaking Brazil, and an independent Haiti and autonomous Quebec of French-speaking peoples, while in South Africa the Dutch acquired practical independence. And political independence, it is hardly necessary to point out, has operated to provide the new nations with special historical traditions at variance not only with one another's but those of parental or primary nationalities in Europe.

Wherefore the nationalities in America—English, Spanish, Portuguese, French—may conveniently be described as secondary, or sub-, nationalities. They have the same languages as their counterparts in Europe, with only dialect differences; but they possess and cherish divergent historical traditions, and a firm will to maintain free and sovereign national states. Special bonds of culture and sympathy survive, of course, between secondary nationalities and their respective primary nationalities. Common language means that Shakespeare, Milton, and Keats are as much a heritage of the people of the United States as of England, and, vice versa, that modern American novels find a large market among Englishmen. It also helps to explain why for almost a century and a half there has been no war between Britain and the United States, why, rather, they have fought side by side in the World Wars of the present century, and are likely to stand together in "cold" or "hot" wars of the future. Likewise, common language, with common literature and customs, contributes to a continuing sympathetic feeling between European Spaniards on the one hand and Spanish Americans and Filipinos on the other, and between Portuguese and Brazilians; and this despite marked racial differences.

The Dominion of Canada contains two secondary nationalities: French Canadian, and English-speaking Canadian; and the latter may conceivably consist of such "tertiary" nationalities as British Canadian and Irish Canadian, for example. Among other self-governing members of the British Commonwealth, Australia and New Zealand have come to comprise a secondary nationality each, while the Union of South Africa includes at least three: Dutch, English, and indigenous Negro.

Further illustrative of the fluidity and complexity of nationality, is the existence of sectionalism, with its tendency to create and preserve separatist variations of dialect and historic tradition and to threaten the unity of a people. In the United States we have had a glaring spectacle of sectionalism and of its issue, a century ago, in a long bloody struggle to break an American "secondary" nationality into two:[1] a Northern States' and a Southern States'; and though political union was preserved and fortified, we all know that a kind of peculiar and "tertiary" American nationality has survived to this day in Dixie.

Furthermore, we should remark here that nationalism as an exalting of nationality is somewhat more artificially stimulated, though no less potent, in a country like the United States than in a European country such as England or France or Sweden or Germany. It is naturally so. In Europe everyone is aware of belonging to a particular nationality with distinguishing language and traditions; and one's nationalism is a relatively normal outgrowth and expression of it. In the United States, on the other hand, where the population consists of descendants of immigrants from a great variety of European nationalities, to say nothing of Negroes and Asiatics and indigenous Indian tribesmen, nationalism is invoked and pressed into service as creator and assurer of a novel and unifying American nationality—a national "melting pot."[2]

[1] See Avery O. Craven's *The Growth of Southern Nationalism, 1848–1861* (1953).

[2] The best treatment of American nationalism is Merle E. Curti's *The Roots of American Loyalty* (1946).

3. Patriotism

Nationality is a fact, and from the dawn of history there has been a multiplicity of nationalities in various stages of development or decline. But until people are conscious of nationality and make it the prime object of their *patriotism*, they do not produce cultural or political nationalism.

What, then, is patriotism? It is "love of country," yes. As "love," it is an emotion, involving fondness, sympathy, fidelity, loyalty. In one form or another, it appears to be instinctive with man, a natural part and essential prop of his gregariousness. It is basic to human life in family, in locality, in society.

Love of country is an aggregate of several kinds of loyalty. It involves a "feline" loyalty to familiar places, a "canine" loyalty to familiar persons, a distinctively human loyalty to familiar ideas and usages. There may be various objects of these combined loyalties— of this patriotism. It may be family or clan or tribe. It may be village or town. It may be a province or an empire or any sort of state. It may be a club or a Masonic lodge or a church. It may be a nationality.

Loyalty to familiar places is relatively natural, but it requires artificial effort—purposeful conscious education and training—to render man loyal to the sum total of places, unfamiliar as well as familiar, in an entire country inhabited by his nationality. In French, distinction is usefully made between *patrie* (one's whole nation or "fatherland") and *pays* (one's immediate homeland). Everybody, besides having a *patrie*, has a *pays*. My own *pays* is New York, particularly the south-central part of Upstate New York. Here I was born and spent my youth. Here five generations of both paternal and maternal ancestors lived and are buried. Here is my true home, along the gently flowing Susquehanna and amid the smiling wooded hills. Hither I resort whenever I can. This *pays* is for me a primary and most natural stimulus of patriotic sentiment and loyalty. Yet I have been taught—and am expected—to extend this sentiment and loyalty to such unfamiliar places as Alaska, North Dakota, Oklahoma and Utah, and at the same time to withhold them from Canada and Mexico.

Similarly, loyalty to familiar persons—to family, friends, and neigh-bors—is natural and usual. But special civic training is required to make a man loyal to the sum total of persons, familiar and unfamiliar, who constitute his whole nationality. And it takes additional training for a man to learn that he should respect and obey, and be patriotic about, national officials who carry on remote from him.

Furthermore, man being man, it is natural for him to be loyal to some ideas and ideals which occur to him and which he thinks good. But most such ideas do not germinate spontaneously within him. Rather, they are carried to, and seeded in him by his fellows. And it necessitates systematic and repeated efforts to implant in the masses of an extended nationality a community of national thought and ideals to which they will be loyal.

Patriotism, therefore, while instinctive in its origin and root, is much more naturally and readily associated with a small community in a restricted area than with a large nationality in a broad expanse of territory. Only through an intensive and extensive educational proc-ess will a local group of people become thoroughly aware of their entire nationality and supremely loyal to it.

The cultural bases of nationality, let me repeat, are a common language and common historical traditions. When these by some process of education become the objects of popular emotional pa-triotism, the result is nationalism.

There are degrees of nationalism, as of any emotion. Our loyalty to nationality and national state may be conditioned by other loyalties —to family, to church, to humanity, to internationalism—and hence restricted in corresponding degree. On the other hand, nationalism may be a paramount, a supreme loyalty, commanding all others. This usually occurs when national emotion is fused with religious emotion, and nationalism itself becomes a religion or a substitute for religion.

CHAPTER II

The Religious Sense

1. Varieties of Religious Experience

Among the traits which characterize man and mark him off from all other creatures—speech, abstract thought, and so on—religion is conspicuous. From the dawn of his history man has been distinguished by what may be called a "religious sense," that is, a faith in some god, some mysterious and controlling power outside of himself, a faith accompanied by feelings of awe and reverence and usually attended by external rites and ceremonies.

Everywhere and under very diverse forms, we find expression of the religious sense—in caves and burial mounds of primitive men; in pyramids and temples of ancient Egypt; in the laws of Moses and the rites of Aaron; in the Greek Olympus, the Roman Pantheon, and the Germanic Valhalla; in the tended fire of vestal virgins and the sacred groves of Celtic druids; in the shrines of Inca and Maya and Aztec; in the taboos of Eskimo and Hottentot and Polynesian. We find it likewise in great religious systems, such as Hinduism, Buddhism, Confucianism, Christianity, and Islam, which through centuries have counted their followers and devotees by billions.

Apparently the religious sense is so ingrained in man that normally he must give expression to it in one way or another. He may lose faith in a particular religion and cease to participate in its cult, but if so he is apt to dedicate himself consciously or unconsciously to another object of reverence and worship. It may be worship of Christ or Buddha. It may be worship of totem or fetish. Or it may be worship

of science or humanity, of abstract "truth" or some particular ideology
—provided these concepts are written in his mind and on his heart
with capital letters. In any case it involves an experience, a reveren-
tial emotion, which is primordially religious.

Even in ages when doubt and skepticism about a popular religion
have been most rampant, the very skeptics and doubters have been
disposed to seek some object outside of themselves to which they
might pay reverence. For example, in the early centuries of the Christian era, when Græco-Roman paganism was losing its hold on the intellectual classes of the Roman Empire, there was a notable tendency
to find an outlet for the religious sense, on the one hand, in Stoicism
and other philosophies that proclaimed a truer higher divinity in duty
or in reasoned pleasure, and, on the other hand, in mystical communion with strange and somewhat bizarre gods, with Isis and
Osiris, with Mithra, or with the "spirits" and "emanations" of Neo-
Platonism. The resultant unsettling and diversification of religion was
in that instance only transitional and not at all irreligious. It inspired
quaint attempts to mingle and reconcile heterogeneous objects of
worship. It presently produced a kind of religious syncretism, and
thereby helped to prepare the way for the eventual widespread diffusion and acceptance of Christianity.

Christianity did not represent a clean break with the religious past.
It was rooted in the antique doctrine and scriptures of Judaism, and
for its developing organization and ritual it owed much to its Græco-
Roman environment. In other words, Christianity was, to a considerable extent, a syncretic religion, as had been the paganism which it
supplanted. Christianity, to be sure, differed fundamentally in theology and in moral teaching from paganism, but both of them, and also
the transitional steps from the latter to the former, appealed to man's
religious sense.

Again, in the later Middle Ages, doubts arose and multiplied in
western and central Europe about certain dogmas and practices of
the Catholic Church. Followed widespread repudiation and denunciation of Catholic Christianity, and rise of Protestantism. But as one
studies historic Protestantism one is impressed less by the novelties

which the reformers introduced into the content of Christianity than by the conservatism with which most of them clung to major doctrines and rites of the older Christian Church. (The reader may recall that long ago this opinion was voiced by Gibbon with devastating rhetoric and mordant wit in the famous twentieth chapter of his *Decline and Fall*.) Those reformers borrowed plentifully from Catholicism, while at the same time they appropriated much from intellectual movements of their day and put themselves especially under new obligations to ancient Judaism. Conversion from Catholicism to Protestantism in the sixteenth century doubtless betokened a lessening faith in a specific religion, but the historical student knows that the sixteenth century, instead of being irreligious, was fanatically religious. In Protestantism, as in Catholicism, or in Judaism, and in transition from one to another, man gave expression to his religious sense.

In like manner it may be argued that the subsequent disintegration of Protestantism into numerous denominations and sects has been a modern parallel to the ancient deliquescence of Græco-Roman paganism, and, further, that the syncretism—the "ecumenical" federation of churches—latterly proceeding in the Protestant world may correspondingly usher in a new type of Christianity which, however Protestant in name, will depart considerably from historic Protestantism. Yet such a neo-Protestantism is likely to differ from its sixteenth century forerunner not so much in its constituent elements as in its adaptations and stresses and results. Above all, it will be, like historic Protestantism, and like historic Catholicism before that, an embodiment of man's religious sense.

The foregoing examples of man's religious sense have been chiefly drawn from the European Western world. Many more could be cited from the Far East and Middle East, from Asia and Africa and Oceania. Indeed, with mankind throughout time and space, a religious sense has been natural and normal. Its universality among primitive tribes has been amply demonstrated by a host of anthropological students and fieldworkers, and summed up in such scholarly works as Clark Wissler's *Man and Culture* and Alfred Kroeber's

Anthropology. And whatever may be the faults and shortcomings of Arnold Toynbee's epic philosophizing about the rise, decline, and fall of civilizations, he makes out a good case for a particular religion's being an essential and distinguishing element in each civilization. Similar views are set forth, as cogently and more simply, in Christopher Dawson's excellent study, *Religion and Culture;* they are adumbrated too in Jacques Maritain's *Philosophy of History.*

2. Applications of the Religious Sense, Especially to Communism and Nationalism

Nowadays a goodly number of people, while admitting that religion has played an important role in the past, would contend that, under the impact of science, technology, and secular education, contemporary man is getting away from religion, away from the "superstition" which religion is said to engender. The contention, I think, is only partly sound; it requires elucidation and radical amendment. It usually concerns the traditional religion of Europe and America, and the alleged loosening hold of Christianity upon intellectuals and the masses. We should bear in mind, however, that throughout the past, even in "ages of faith," many baptized Christians were notoriously lacking in Christian piety and devotion, and that there are probably more sincere, practicing Christians today than ever before, and certainly greater missionary activity.

Yet we must admit that while the bulk of our European ancestors, regardless of nationality or class, at least professed the Christian faith and accepted the Christian ethic as the standard of conduct, this holds true no longer. For two and a half centuries, an increasing number of European and American intellectuals and would-be intellectuals (there is a difference) have been repudiating or ignoring the Christian religious heritage. Moreover, with the advent and spread of the Industrial Revolution during the last century and a half, the masses have been uprooted not only from ancestral home but from ancestral religion, and large segments of them in Europe have become quite indifferent to Christianity if not actively hostile to it.

Thereby a kind of religious void has been created for large numbers of people in modern Europe and the contemporary world. But, as I have suggested above, any such void is unnatural, and an urge arises to fill the void with some new faith. Intellectuals have found this in "scientism," in "humanitarianism," in "positivism," in "freemasonry," to one or another of which they evince a single-minded and at least quasi-religious devotion. To be sure, these objects are likely to be too abstract, too esoteric, for mass adoration. As the masses grow cold about the historic Christian faith and practice, they have tended, rather, to accept other and more attractive substitutes offered them by intellectuals, most notable of which are communism and nationalism.

Communism, since the days of Karl Marx a century ago, and especially since the Russian Revolution of 1917, has had a distinctly religious, as well as economic, appeal. Though avowedly materialist and atheistic, it promises an earthly paradise. It has its saints and martyrs, its doctors and heretics. It is zealously propagandist and demands of its adherents an exclusive and unswerving loyalty. In the Kremlin it now possesses a curious kind of central authority, in nature at once political and religious, imperial and quasi-papal. It is intolerant of any rival religion, particularly of Christianity, and it looks confidently forward to conquering the world.

Yet we may doubt whether Marxian or Leninist communism would have the position and influence it now has, or threaten to become the world religion of the future, if it had not latterly exploited and been reenforced by another emotional substitute for traditional supernatural religion: namely, nationalism. Nationalism has a warmth and a pietistic character which communism lacks. It is not so coldly and impersonally materialist. It has a spiritual quality; and, unlike communism, it appreciates the basic religious truth that man does not live by bread alone. Hence the emotion which nationalism arouses is likely to be shared to the full not only by an elite but by the mass of common people. Furthermore, nationalism usually gives some satisfaction, which communism scarcely can, to man's craving for immortality and for freedom. At any rate, it relates man to his nation's historic past and identifies him and his descendants with the future life of the nation. And its goal is the assurance of freedom and individuality and autonomy, if not to the person, at least to one's nationality and national state.

Karl Marx was not a nationalist. Although he had a special regard for his German fatherland, he spent most of his life away from it and was preeminently a cosmopolite. He thought that large states were preferable to small ones based on nationality. Though himself of Jewish background, he surely would have had no sympathy with Zionism or with Israel. His clarion call was, "Workers of all nations, unite!"

Nevertheless, after Marx's death his Socialist following tended more and more to seek popular support by espousing national patriotism and the principle of nationality. We merely recall, in this connection, such "revisionist" Socialist leaders prior to World War I as Eduard Bernstein in Germany and Jean Jaurès in France. In both World Wars of our century, the vast majority of Socialists proved themselves less loyal to Marx than to their respective national states.

3. Religio-Nationalist Communism

Lenin, during his years of exile from his native Russia, earned the reputation of being a left-wing Marxian, with only minor concern for nationalism. He remained, of course, after the successful Bolshevik Revolution of 1917 which he headed, and until his death in 1924, a convinced and zealous exponent of dictatorial communism. But in order to meet pressing economic problems and to cope with national opposition, he showed a willingness to compromise with capitalism on the one hand and with nationalism on the other. In the latter case he established the office of "Commissar of Nationalities" and entrusted it to his friend and colleague, Joseph Stalin. On one point, that of historic supernatural religion, Lenin was uncompromising. With quasi-religious fanaticism, he persecuted the Christian churches and made atheism the official state creed. After his death, ironically enough, Lenin's body was carefully embalmed like an Egyptian pharaoh's on its way to eternal life, and in its glass mausoleum in the

Red Square of Moscow it has since been exposed and venerated as though it were the incorruptible body of a Christian saint.

Stalin, as is well known, belonged to the Georgian nationality, and he combined with his devotion to communism a special regard for the non-Russian nationalities within the Russian domain. As Commissar of Nationalities under Lenin, he was instrumental in providing, by the constitution of 1922, for the transformation of the centralized empire of the Tsars into the "Union of Soviet Socialist Republics," each "republic" comprising a particular nationality—Ukrainian, Byelorussian, Georgian, and Armenian, as well as Russian proper (Great Russian)—and each, though politically dominated by the central Communist party, constituting a cultural entity. Subsequently, after Stalin succeeded Lenin in supreme command at Moscow, he reaffirmed and broadened the principle of cultural autonomy by adding to the Union "republics" for tribal peoples in Asiatic Russia: Uzek, Turkmen, Tadzhik, Kirghiz, and so on. Paradoxically, the encouragement Stalin thus gave to the preservation and development of local languages and traditions—and to the local pride that went with them—did much to promote popular loyalty throughout the Soviet Union to the dictatorship at Moscow.

In other respects, the Communist dictatorship under Stalin took on a nationalist complexion. He certainly did not allow the state to "wither away," as Marx had foretold it would under communism. Rather, he exalted it and rendered it as authoritarian and despotic as any extreme nationalist, say a Mussolini or a Hitler, could have desired. More significant, he identified the interests of the international proletariat with the national interests of Russia and fostered a mounting distrust of the West, its imperialism and its internationalism.

Then, too, in his later years, perhaps drunk with power, Stalin accepted and abetted the public worship of himself as a national hero and demigod. Everywhere in Russian homes his portraits replaced, or were hung beside, the old Christian icons, and the fulsomeness of his praise and adulation reached its climax in a veritable apotheosis on the occasion of his seventieth birthday in 1949. When he died four years later he was appropriately embalmed and enshrined alongside of Lenin. True, his personal cult was reduced by a dictatorial successor, but not his achievement of infusing Russian communism—and imperialism—with the spirit of nationalism.

In the current world, we have innumerable examples of how the Russian dictatorship perseveres in serving its own ends by denouncing Western imperialism and fomenting native nationalism—in the Far East, in the Middle and Near East, in Africa, in Latin America. It expects, of course, to bring resulting "freed" nationalities into a vastly expanded Union of Soviet Socialist Republics with continuing capital and dominance at Moscow. For this end the Russians are obviously a "chosen people," and Moscow the "Rome" of the future. All of which represents quite a departure from the prophetic "scientific" teachings of Karl Marx.

The new gospel presents some difficulties. Peoples aspiring to national independence in Asia and Africa may not be content with the cultural nationalism which the Russian dictatorship would grant them; they are apt to strive for political nationalism as well. Nor, in the long run, are they likely, after rejecting Western imperialism, to welcome a Russian imperialism. Nationalism, after all, now appears to be wider in scope than communism, and more universally motivating. It is more capable of arousing a religious sense, both popular and impelling.

To sum up, man's religious sense is exemplified not only in great surviving religions such as Christianity, Hinduism, Buddhism, and Islam, and in the animism and pagan cults of primitive peoples, but in contemporary communism and especially in modern nationalism. Let me stress, however, that there are variant kinds and degrees of nationalism. Some can be reconciled or allied with historical supernatural religion. Others can be utilized to give quasi-religious sanction to an intrinsically materialist and atheistic movement like communism. Still others can be religions in themselves, mutually jealous and exclusive.

It is the development of this last type of nationalism with which we shall here be primarily concerned. We shall note, as we go, that in its original form nationalism was simply an expression of tribalism, that then it declined and was displaced by broader loyalties, that its resurrection occurred in modern times and among traditionally Christian peoples, that its full flowering in the West and its implanting elsewhere have been relatively recent.

CHAPTER III

Primitive Nationalism
and Its Long Submergence

1. Tribalism

All Europeans and Americans, and so far as I know all other humans, are descended, more or less distantly, from primitive tribesmen. In the dim background of our Western civilization, we have heard of ancient tribes of Greece and Italy, of twelve tribes of Israel, of Celtic tribes tiresomely enumerated by Julius Caesar, and of names of a bewildering variety of Germanic tribes—Ostrogoths and Visigoths, Alemans, Angles, Burgundians, Franks, Gepids, Lombards, Marcomans, Saxons, Swabians, Vandals. There were at least as many ancient Slavic tribes, and there were, too, those galloping, terrorizing tribes of Avars, Huns, and Mongols. Clan life, that is, tribal life, long endured in Ireland and Scotland; and England was once upon a time a heptarchy of tribal states. Our American Indians and Negroes issue from tribes, the one indigenous, the other African, many of which still exist and furnish rich material for contemporary anthropologists.

Tribalism was, and wherever it survives still is, a primitive, small-scale, and usually intensive type of nationalism. Clark Wissler, among other anthropological scholars, has made it abundantly clear that each tribe speaks a distinctive language or dialect. As he says, an "important tribal characteristic . . . is speech; for, wherever a difference in speech is found, one may at once suspect a tribal distinction. A complete classification of peoples according to speech will reveal the tribal grouping."[1] Each tribe likewise has its own distinctive traditions and cultural pattern; and it follows some peculiar routine and ritual in indoctrinating its youth and admitting them to full membership. An amusing, as well as enlightening account of such an initiation was provided some years ago by Elizabeth Weber concerning an African tribe quaintly entitled the *Duk-Duks*. And, of course, each tribe customarily has its little army of "braves," with whom it engages in intertribal war, for war seems to be a pretty constant avocation of mankind, whether primitive or modern.

Above all, each tribe normally possesses a distinctive and pretty localized religion. As Lord Bryce noticed a half century ago: "Men with little knowledge of each other, with no experience of wide political union, held differences . . . to be natural and irremovable barriers. . . . Religion appeared to them a matter purely local; and as there were gods of the hills and gods of the valleys, of the land and of the sea, so each tribe rejoiced in its peculiar deities, looking on the natives of other countries who worshipped other gods as Gentiles, natural foes, unclean beings. Such feelings . . . frequently show themselves in the early records of Greece and Italy: in Homer the hero who wanders over the unfruitful sea glories in sacking the cities of the stranger; the primitive Latins have the same word for a foreigner and an enemy."

Tribes and tribalism are characteristic of the earliest ages and the most diverse areas of which we have any record. They probably were prevalent throughout countless centuries and millenniums of prehistory: in other words, during the greater part of mankind's existence on the earth.

2. Submergence of Tribalism: Military and Religious Factors

Yet for fairly long periods, and to greater or lesser degree, man has broken out of narrow tribal confines and transformed tribalism into broader loyalties. For the intense loyalty of primitive man to his tribe, and his seemingly innate hostility to "foreigners," did not

[1] *Man and Culture*, pp. 48–49. See also Alfred L. Kroeber's *Anthropology: Race, Language, Culture, Psychology, Prehistory*, rev. ed. (1948).

preclude a curiosity on his part about alien tribesmen and peoples or a desire to exchange goods with them or a willingness to borrow elements of their culture and even on occasion to federate with them. A famous example of this was the Iroquois Confederacy of American Indian tribes. And with advancing and spreading civilization, tribalism, that is, primitive nationalism, tended in various parts of the world to be pushed into the background. It ceased to command the supreme loyalty, the supreme patriotism, of civilized men.

What submerged that early nationalism, and long kept it submerged, was one or another (usually a combination) of *four* factors: One was the conquest of various tribes by a military leader who forced them into a military and political (and economic) union. Thereby was created a military empire which, if it had a line of able and lucky rulers, would outlast the conqueror who had originally founded it and would gradually evolve a system of administration, laws, and education for its consolidation and perpetuation. Whence arose, in place of tribal patriotism, or atop it, an imperial patriotism—a patriotism applied to an empire and its head.

Plentiful examples are furnished by ancient empires of Egypt, Assyria, Babylonia, Persia, India, and China, and, in pre-Columbian America, by the Aztec empire of Mexico and the Inca empire of Peru. There were also Alexander the Great's far-flung empire and its succeeding offshoots, to which were subjected not only Greek tribes and cities but Egyptians and disparate peoples of Asia Minor, Syria, and the Balkans.

But the outstanding example, so far as Europe is concerned, was the Roman Empire, which, in addition to Greeks and other peoples of Alexander the Great's empire, embraced Etruscans, Latin and Italian tribes, Carthaginians, Iberians, Gauls, Berbers, Armenians, Jews, Britons, and tribes of Germans and Slavs. Undoubtedly the variegated population of the Roman Empire was conscious of belonging to this or that nationality; yet for centuries loyalty to the empire seems to have generally transcended loyalty to the several nationalities within the empire. The only nationalist revolt of note was that of the Jews in the first century A.D.; it was forcibly suppressed, and both before and afterward many a Jew adopted Hellenic or Roman culture. St. Paul, the Christian apostle to the Gentiles, was proud of being a Roman citizen as well as belonging to the Jewish nation.

So great, too, was the fame and prestige of the Roman Empire that, at least in name, it lasted in central Europe until 1806, and, as the Austrian Empire under the Habsburgs, until 1919. It actually continued in the East, as the Byzantine Empire, until Constantinople fell to the Turks in 1453; and the succeeding Ottoman Empire, which was patterned largely after it, survived until 1920. Even in modern and recent times, when nationalism has again become commonplace and ubiquitous, repeated attempts have been made to satisfy imperial ambitions and hankerings—by Napoleon, by Mussolini and Hitler, by Stalin and Khrushchev and Mao Tse-tung.

A second, and very important, factor in submerging tribalism was the growth and spread of a religion from some particular tribe or nationality to others. Thus issued forth so-called "world religions," carrying and establishing a widespread community of beliefs, worship, usages, law, and culture, and in certain cases something resembling a theocratic state. The construction of military empires, just mentioned, was usually accompanied and sustained by a fusing of tribal gods and rites into an imperial pantheon, with supreme divinity and worship being attributed to the emperor. This occurred, as is well known, in the common paganism and emperor-worship of the ancient Roman Empire, and something of the sort marked the development of Hinduism under the Maurya empire of ancient India, and similarly the state religions of Aztec and Inca empires. Confucianism, too, in its exalting of the ruler proved a valuable support for the upbuilding and maintenance of the Chinese Empire. As for ancient Japan, its native religion of Shinto, though remaining essentially tribal and local, inculcated one unifying belief—that the emperors were descended from a sun goddess and hence entitled to homage as chief priests and divinities.

On occasion a great and magnetic teacher has appeared and

started a religious movement that has spread from one people to others and on beyond any particular empire. That was the case with Buddhism which, beginning with the teaching of Gautama Buddha in India in the fifth century B.C., became the prevailing religion of Ceylon, Burma, Siam, Indo-China, and Tibet, and won multitudes of converts in China and Japan. Above all it was the case with both Christianity and Islam.

The one, the gospel of the God-Man, Jesus Christ, originally appeared as an offshoot of tribal Judaism, but it was embodied in an organization—the Christian Church—which followed the injunction of the Founder "to preach the gospel to all nations." Its apostles and missionaries won a gradually increasing number of converts throughout the Roman Empire, despite spasmodic forceful efforts of the pagan emperors to suppress it. In less than four hundred years it supplanted Græco-Roman paganism as the dominant and official religion of the Empire and was already extending its missionary enterprise to barbaric tribesmen beyond the Empire's northern limits. Thus in time a Christianized "European" community was expanded from the Mediterranean over Celts and Germans and Slavs and Magyars and Finns, and eventually across the Atlantic to Americans and even across the Pacific to Filipinos.

Islam similarly sprang from amidst Arab tribalism, but the Prophet Mohammed did not confine himself to reforming customary local religion at Mecca and Medina. His appeal was universal and militant, and, like Christianity, Islam was carried far afield—across the northern breadth of Africa, all over southwestern and central Asia, into India and Indonesia, and temporarily into Spain and the Balkans. As Christianity was distinctive of Western civilization, so was Islam of the civilization of Near and Middle East.

For centuries these two religions were so influential that, with millions of human beings in their respective areas of the world, the most natural grouping seemed to be not tribal or national but Christian or Muslim, and the paramount object of patriotism not any national state but Christendom or Islam. The only great wars of the European Middle Ages were the crusades, those protracted struggles from the eleventh to the sixteenth century between Christians and Muslims. In this connection, we may also recall the intra-Christian civil wars which raged in Germany from 1520 to 1650: they clearly indicated that the loyalty of the German participants was less to the German nationality or German empire than to Protestantism or to the Catholic Church.

3. Linguistic and Economic Factors

We have now discussed two factors which contributed to the submergence of primitive nationalism, that is, of tribalism: (1) the rise of international military empires; (2) the spread of international "world" religions. A *third* factor was linguistic and literary.

Languages were spoken long before any of them were written. Each primitive tribe, as we have seen, had a distinctive spoken language or dialect, and every member of the tribe presumably spoke it as well, or as badly, as every other member. It was a primary aid to tribal solidarity. In time, however, this or that language became literary; it was written. We can hardly exaggerate the importance of this step. The invention and use of some form of writing meant the drawing of a line between prehistory and history. It enabled scribes to supplement oral tradition by keeping and handing down a record of tribal exploits. It made it possible to intensify education and indoctrination of youth by written as well as by spoken instruction.

At first thought, these effects might seem to favor an increase, not a lessening, of tribal solidarity and nationalism. We should bear in mind, nevertheless, that, for centuries, writing was learned and practiced by a minority of persons, not by a majority; the masses could not read or write. Hence between the literate and the illiterate a cleavage appeared. The former developed a fairly rigorous literary language. The latter continued to use a looser and more familiar "vernacular." Then, with the establishment of extensive empires or religious communities, the literary language of a particular people would normally become the literary language of such an empire or community, and thereby the cleavage would be accentuated between a literary language and a variety of vernaculars, and the vernaculars would be despised by the educated and upper classes.

In this way, Greek as a literary language, following the conquests of Alexander the Great and accompanying the early Christian missions, overlaid many a vernacular of southeastern Europe and of the Asian and African "Near East." The Founder of Christianity commonly spoke Aramaic, a Semitic dialect, but the earliest written records we have of Him are the Greek epistles of St. Paul and the gospels and other books of the New Testament in Greek. Likewise, Jewish scholars at Alexandria in Egypt prepared the famous Septuagint, a Greek version of the Hebrew Old Testament, and both Philo and Josephus were Hellenized Jews.

In like manner, Latin, originally the speech of Italian tribes, became the literary language of Rome and all its western provinces, and thence of the whole of Western Christendom. Similarly, Arabic, as the language of the Koran, the sacred scriptures of the Prophet Mohammed, became a common vehicle of Muslim writers throughout most of the Islamic world. Literary Chinese attended the spread of Confucianism over the Chinese empire. Literary Sanskrit provided the great classics of India and the Hindu religion. Among literate persons such widely diffused languages militated against nationalism and in favor of a sort of cosmopolitan patriotism, a sense of belonging to cultural societies that overlapped tribes and nationalities.

Let us now turn to the fourth and final factor in submerging tribalism—the economic. Primitive tribes had a primitive and mainly self-contained economy. They might engage in barter with their neighbors, or they might get what they wanted by raiding or fighting them. But with advance of agricultural and industrial arts, with domestication of animals and plants, irrigation, and expanding use of copper, iron, boats, and wagons, economic development overleaped tribal borders and rendered easier and more natural the founding and expansion of empires, the spread and propagation of "world" religions, and diffusion of literary languages and cosmopolitan culture.

In the expanding economy, however, both industrial specialization and economic inequality became more pronounced and customary. Besides, they gave rise to changed human groupings, which, in turn, through training and accumulating tradition, came to command new and enduring loyalties. *One* was the *city-state,* dominated usually by a commercial aristocracy, with subordinate artisans and guildsmen, and with subject servants and slaves. Such were the ancient Phœnician city-states of Tyre and Sidon and Carthage, or the Greek city-states of Athens, Sparta, Corinth, and Syracuse. Such, also, were the city-states of medieval Italy, Germany, and the Netherlands: Venice, Genoa, Florence; Lübeck, Hamburg, Augsburg; Antwerp, Bruges, and Ghent. City-states differed widely from primitive tribes, and yet contained only portions of this or that linguistic nationality. Their inhabitants normally evinced an ardent patriotism, but it was not the nationalism of tribesmen nor that of modern peoples. It was local urban patriotism. It was urbanism, rather than nationalism, and the prevalent kind of war in which city-states engaged, whether between Athens and Sparta, or between Genoa and Venice, was not intertribal or international, but interurban.

Second was the *provincial estate,* chiefly agricultural, with quasi-independent noble landlord, with knightly aides and military retainers, and with a laboring peasantry. This, like the city-state, was intermediate between tribe and empire, or between tribe and modern nationality. In Europe, for example, it existed in the Roman Empire and characterized the feudalism of the Middle Ages. Outside, it was long commonplace in India and in Japan. It is represented by English titles like duchy, barony, province, county, and so forth. Under it, one's chief loyalty was to *pays* rather than to *patrie;* it was provincial or feudal, rather than nationalist.

4. Continuing National Consciousness

I do not mean to imply from the foregoing that popular consciousness of nationality was utterly blotted out by military empires, world religions, supranational languages and literatures, or economic developments. Not at all. It was submerged, but not destroyed.

In Europe, for instance, the Roman Empire recognized the continuing existence within it of a variety of peoples speaking languages or dialects different from literary Latin and retaining peculiar customs and traditions, and for them it evolved a special system of law—the *jus gentium,* the law of tribes, or peoples—differing from the legal system for full-fledged imperial citizens. Likewise the Catholic Christian Church, while intent upon safeguarding unity of faith and morals and its supreme spiritual authority, generally respected the sensibilities of peoples it converted by establishing primatial sees for each, and initiating vernacular literatures through translation of Bible and prayer books from Latin or Greek.

A goodly number of examples of national pride, national rivalry, and national patriotism can be cited from the annals of medieval Europe. Let me mention a few. The separation, in the fifth century, of Armenian and Egyptian Coptic Christians from the Catholic Church and the Greek Orthodox schism of the eleventh century were results as much of national feeling as of doctrinal divergence. There are recurrent references in medieval French literature to such patriotic phrases as *la belle France* and *la douce France.* At the start of the Second Crusade in 1147, the French army of Louis VII and the German army of Conrad III were kept separate lest they battle each other instead of the Muslims. The Albigensian Crusade of the thirteenth century, though ostensibly religious, pitted French against Provençal; and the Hundred Years' War, beginning as a feudal and dynastic struggle, ended in the fifteenth century as an international war between French and English. In the same century, the Catholic General Council of Constance substituted voting by "nations" for traditional individual voting; and conflict between national-conscious Germans on the one hand and national-conscious Slavs on the other hand was signalized by the Polish victory at Tannenberg, by the erection of the Czech university at Prague, and by the Hussite wars.

Yet after making liberal allowance for these and other evidences of nationalism in the Middle Ages, the fact remains, as I see it from my reading of history, that nationalism throughout that period was spasmodic rather than continuous and that it was inferior in strength and influence to other human loyalties. If anybody in Europe is asked now who or what he is, his response is almost certain to be: "I'm English," or "I'm Irish," or "I'm German" or "Italian" or "Russian" or some other national. If a medieval European had been asked the same question, he probably would have answered: "I'm a Christian."

Modern political nationalism, as I have already mentioned and shall later explain, is European in formation and development. But well into the sixteenth century most of Europe itself was characterized by two quite different trends, neither of which was nationalistic. One was a supranational cosmopolitanism or universalism, represented by Christian religion and Catholic Church, by regard for empire as the highest type of political state, and by use of Latin as the common language of scholars and intellectuals whether they were at Paris, Oxford, Rome, Mainz, Salamanca, Coimbra, Prague, Budapest, or Upsala, and regardless of the vernaculars they might speak. The other was an infranational localism, which was especially marked among the peasant masses, who lived in the same limited area for generations and expended their loyalty on parish church, on local village, on feudal lord, and which was similarly marked among urban dwellers whose patriotism centered in city, guild, and cathedral.

CHAPTER IV

Roots of Modern Nationalism in Christendom, Particularly in England

1. Vernacular Languages and Literatures

Four developments, representing a curious inversion of the factors which had operated to submerge primitive tribal nationalism, served in late Middle Ages and early modern times to resuscitate national feeling in Europe and to initiate the large-scale nationalism with which we are familiar today. These were: (1) the rise of vernacular literatures and relative decline of Latin, attended by waning of cosmopolitanism among intellectuals and waxing of national cultures; (2) the emergence of the monarchical national state, as a political institution stronger and more efficient than feudal or city state, or surviving relic of the Roman Empire; (3) transformation of guild or manorial local economy into a national-state economy, with resultant national regulation of commerce, industry, and agriculture; (4) disruption of Catholic Christendom and establishment of national churches.

Greek and especially Latin had long been the predominant literary languages of European nationalities. Of course, side by side with them, there persisted or developed national languages—the so-called vernaculars—among which were tongues, such as Basque, Gaelic, and Breton, that antedated and survived the diffusion of Latin and Greek; others, such as French, Italian, Castilian, Catalan, and Portuguese, that gradually grew out of Latin dialects; and still others, such as Teutonic, Slavic, Finnish, and Magyar, that derived from tribal "barbarian" speech; and finally the peculiar mixture of German and French that we call English. But literary production in these vernaculars was at first relatively slight in quantity, and religious more than national in content; even the requisite alphabets and forms of letters were borrowed and adapted from Latin or, in eastern Europe, from Greek.

In central and western Europe, the cultural area of Catholic Christianity, all educated persons throughout the Middle Ages knew Latin as well as their native tongue. For instance, Erasmus, the foremost scholar of the early sixteenth century, was a Dutchman by birth, and Dutch was his mother tongue, but his mastery of Latin rendered him quite cosmopolitan: he lived among educated Frenchmen, Englishmen, Italians, Germans, and Belgians, with all of whom he freely talked and corresponded in Latin; he lectured for a while in Latin at the Collège de France; he wrote Latin letters to the Pope, to the Kings of England, France, and Spain, to his famous publisher at Venice, and to his numerous critics in all parts of Europe.

Before the time of Erasmus, however—at least from the thirteenth century—a multiplying number of schools and universities in Catholic Christendom had been spreading literacy and formal education as preparation for careers not only in the church but also in law, medicine, and other secular professions. Thereby a market for secular writing in the vernacular was created or enlarged. The response was particularly early and noteworthy in Italy. In the early 1200's, while Italian troubadours were composing love lyrics at the court of Frederick II in Sicily, Saint Francis of Assisi in Tuscany was writing his sacred canticles, followed soon by those lovely legends of the Saint, *The Little Flowers*, which fixed the Tuscan dialect as the literary form of vernacular Italian. A century later, Dante used Latin for his controversial political writings, but Tuscan Italian for his immortal *Divine Comedy*, and Petrarch, while using polished Latin for his epistles, employed vernacular Italian for his famed sonnets. By the 1500's Machiavelli, Boccaccio, Ariosto, and Tasso were composing their masterpieces in Italian.

By this time, similar vernacular literatures were flourishing among the English (Chaucer was a contemporary of Dante, and Shakespeare of Tasso), the Germans, the French, the Provençal-Catalans, the Castilians, the Portuguese, the Norse, and were beginning among Czechs and Poles. Three events of the fifteenth and sixteenth centuries forwarded the process. One was the attempt of humanists of the Renaissance to "purify" Latin of its medieval developments, which had been in the direction of greater simplicity, and to restore ancient classical Latin with its involved sentence structure and its complicated grammar. The attempt was essentially pedantic and did much in the long run to discourage the employment of Latin as a living literary language and to restrict its use to the classroom, to ecclesiastical services, and, for a time, to theological and scientific treatises.

A second aid to the vernaculars was the invention, in the second half of the fifteenth century, of printing and its rapid dissemination throughout Catholic Christendom. It tended to stereotype the common spoken languages, to fix for each a norm of literary usage, and to render possible a cheaper and broader circulation of vernacular literature within a particular nationality. The third aid to the same end was the religious upheaval of the sixteenth century, in the course of which the Protestant Reformers sought popular support by utilizing vernaculars for translations of the Bible, pamphlet propaganda, apologias, and controversial writings; and the Catholics replied in kind.

The development of vernacular literature exalted nationality, for not even a well educated person could be expected to know all the spoken languages, and the large majority of Europeans were familiar only with the language of their own nationality. Writers in English naturally stressed what was peculiar to England, French writers did the same for France, and Italian writers for Italy. National characters were imaginatively depicted, and national aspirations voiced. In the sixteenth century, Machiavelli made eloquent national appeals to the Italians, Camoëns celebrated glorious national exploits of the Portuguese, Luther addressed stirring patriotic letters to the Germans, Cervantes played fancifully with Don Quixote and

Sancho Panza types of Spanish character, and Shakespeare glorified England:

> "This happy breed of men, this little world,
> This precious stone set in the silver sea."

From Shakespeare's day to the present, some "little world" has been echoed and reechoed in epic, drama, ode, history, essay, and novel. National literature has everywhere tended to accentuate what is peculiar to a linguistic group rather than what is characteristic of broader cultural groupings or of the world at large.

2. National States and National Economy

Literary differentiation of nationalities was accompanied in early modern times, in Europe and more especially in western Europe, by political differentiation, that is, by the erection of sovereign national states. This was the achievement primarily of a succession of able and ambitious monarchs in England, France, Spain, Portugal, Scandinavia, and the Dutch Netherlands (where, however, it was not, strictly speaking, a monarch, but rather a princely rebel backed by burgesses). The Tudor dynasty in England, the Valois and Bourbon kings of France, the Habsburgs in Spain, the Avizes in Portugal, the Vasas in Sweden, the Orange family in Holland were, as a rule, strong-willed and determined to be masters in their respective realms. On the one hand they would admit of no overlordship by alien emperor, and they would limit, if not repudiate, any outside ecclesiastical authority. On the other hand they would repress their feudal vassals—dukes, counts, and barons—and any other domestic foes of centralized government. In realizing their goals, they were assisted by the change in methods of warfare which the use of firearms brought about, by the revival of Roman civil law and resulting superior legal talent in their service, and by the interested cooperation of many of their subjects. The upshot was the building and consolidation of fairly large, relatively homogeneous, and definitely independent states in western Europe—England, France, Spain, Portugal, Sweden, Denmark, and the Dutch Netherlands.

That these states were based on nationality is attributable less to design on the part of their monarchs than to chance. It was a fortune of war that obliged English monarchs in the fifteenth century to abandon their dominion in France and to devote their energies to Britain. It was a marriage alliance which united Spain under Ferdinand and Isabella; and another which joined Brittany with France. Generally speaking, European monarchs of the sixteenth, seventeenth, and eighteenth centuries waged wars, in large part, for family reasons, either to place a member of a particular royal house on the throne of another country, or to obtain richer inheritances for their wives and children. Nor were they at all scrupulous about confining their ambitions to peoples of their own language and nationality. They frequently conquered territory inhabited by "foreigners," and they bartered peoples to and fro like cattle.

Yet despite such extranational and dynastic transactions, each of the monarchs of western Europe did include as the core and chief element of his dominion a people speaking a common language, or who learned to use it. In Spain, for example, Castilian, under royal tutelage, became the national language, while Catalan, Basque, and Galician were reduced to the status of secondary languages or "dialects." In France, French was promoted at the expense of Provençal and Breton. In Britain, English was preferred to Welsh and Gaelic. Altogether, loyalty to king was associated with, and proved a stimulus to, popular consciousness of nationality.

It is significant that the great transoceanic expansion of European commerce and economy which occurred at the close of the Middle Ages was closely related to the rise of national states along the Atlantic seaboard. It was rulers and citizens of Portugal, Spain, the Netherlands, France, and England who patronized novel voyages of exploration and discovery, who colonized the American continents and other distant places, and who profited most by overseas trade and exploitation. And the effects in the economic differentiation of nationalities and the growth of national patriotism have been striking.

Previously, as we have noted, the principal units of economic life had been, not national states, but city-states. Now, such localism was subordinated to the theory and practice of economic nationalism, to what is called national mercantilism. The government of every national state sought to make it a self-sufficing economic entity, and to this end various measures were taken. Foreign importation was prohibited or protectively taxed. Domestic production was fostered by bounties or other means. Colonies were sought and drawn into the monopolistic commercial system of the mother country. National navies were built and utilized for the protection and forceful extension of national trade.

National mercantilism was supported by, and in turn it heightened, national patriotism. It certainly fed the dislike and jealousy of rival national states, as indicated by a wealthy French merchant's diatribe in 1615 against English and Dutch competitors: "These foreigners," he wrote, "are leeches who attach themselves to France, gorge themselves on its richest blood, and then drop off. They are lice who suck its juices until they grow burstingly fat. . . ."[1] It likewise provoked a series of international commercial and colonial wars, for as an Anglican Archbishop of Canterbury quaintly observed in the seventeenth century: "In all the Strugglings and Disputes that have of late years befallen this corner of the World, I found, that although the pretence was fine and Spiritual, yet the ultimate end and true scope, was Gold, and Greatness, and Secular Glory."

Indeed, as prosaic dynastic wars in Europe came to be attended by more colorful fighting on the high seas and in fantastic lands beyond the seas, national patriotism responded to a new and potent stimulus. To people in every national state a galaxy of national heroes appeared—hardy mariners and daring discoverers, conquistadores and padres, smugglers and pirates and bold buccaneers, fighters on sea and land. Even the financial profits which accrued to monarch, courtiers, and other privileged individuals were deemed assets of the nation as a whole, and it seemed but meet and right that any successful economic undertaking abroad should be patriotically applauded at home and forcefully protected by one's national state.

[1] Quoted by Charles W. Cole in *French Mercantilist Doctrines Before Colbert* (1930).

3. Religious Revolt and Reform

Finally, as a climactic factor in the development of modern nationalism, there was the religious upheaval of the sixteenth century.
The rising regard for nationality was in part the cause of the Protestant Revolution, and this Revolution, and the Catholic Reformation
in only lesser degree, further stimulated national spirit. One cannot
understand why religious reformers secured the numerous and widespread popular following they did unless one is aware of the national
patriotic appeals which Luther made to Germans, John Knox to
Scotsmen, and Kings of England and Scandinavia to their several
peoples. Nor can one appreciate how the Catholic Church managed
to retain a hold upon so many peoples without knowing of the special
favors the papacy accorded to national sovereigns, notably to those
of Spain, Portugal, and France.

The national results of the upheaval were impressive. The
Protestant Revolution, by disrupting the Catholic Church and
subjecting the Christian community to national variations of form
and substance, dissolved much of the intellectual and moral cement
which had long held European peoples together. At the same time
it gave religious sanction to the notion, already latent, that each people, and each alone, possessed a pure faith and a divine mission. The
so-called religious wars of the sixteenth and seventeenth centuries,
though by no means exclusively religious in origin or outcome, were
popular because they were fought in the name of religion and for
an allegedly national religious ideal; and they surely engendered a
livelier sense of national patriotism. Adherence to the Calvinist Reformed Faith united the northern Netherlands in rebellion against
the Catholic King of Spain, and the long conflict which they waged
against him brought them not only independence but a sturdy Dutch
nationalism. Then, too, the general acceptance of Lutheranism by
Scandinavians exalted the national monarchies of Denmark and
Sweden, and rendered the latter the special crusading champion of
Protestantism on the Continent. In England Protestantism assumed
from the start a national form: national monarchs established the

Anglican Church, and national patriotism sustained it. When, for a variety of reasons—economic and political, as well as religious— Philip II of Spain sent his Grand Armada against England in 1588, the English people rallied wholeheartedly to the support of "Good Queen Bess," and the Armada's defeat has ever since been hailed as a glorious victory equally for English Protestantism and for the English nation.

In Protestant countries Catholics were generally regarded as un- patriotic because they did not prize the religious beliefs and worship of the majority of their fellow countrymen. This was one of the reasons why Catholics suffered persecution at the hands of Protes- tants, and, similarly, why Protestants were persecuted in Catholic countries. For Catholicism was as much a symbol of national pa- triotism in Spain and France as was Protestantism in England or Sweden. Moreover, retention of the Catholic faith by Irishmen at the very time when Englishmen became Protestant served to widen between the two nationalities the difference which the diffusion of the English language and the decline of Gaelic had promised to bridge. The Poles, too, found in Catholicism a guarantee of their continuing national differentiation from Protestant Germans to the west and Orthodox Russians to the east. Incidentally, impetus to Russian nationalism was supplied by the Tsar's erection in 1589 of a national Orthodox patriarchate at Moscow independent of the "ecumenical" Greek patriarchate at Constantinople.

The religious upheaval of the sixteenth century had certain special effects on developing nationalism. One was the popular cult of religio- nationalist heroes such as Philip II, Don Juan, and Alba, among Span- iards; Elizabeth, Drake, and Raleigh, among Englishmen; William of Orange, among Dutchmen; Henry of Navarre, among Frenchmen; Gustavus Vasa and Gustavus Adolphus, among Swedes; John So- bieski, among Poles. Another was the increased power of national monarchs through confiscation of church lands, exercise of authority previously exercised by the papacy, and establishment of control over the local clergy. A third special effect, closely related to the second, was "secularization," or what the French call *étatisme*. It was subor- dination of church to state, as the nominally Catholic Machiavelli and the Protestant Erastus alike urged in the sixteenth century, and the transference of responsibility for education and charity from church to state—a transference made first and foremost in Protestant nations.

4. England the Seat of Modern Nationalism

All four factors just discussed—linguistic, political, economic, and religious—did not operate with equal force in the countries and among the nationalities of Christendom. Consider, for example, Germany and the Germans. Here a vernacular national literature developed, but not a national state, or a national economy, or a comprehensive national church. Plenty of national spirit was exhibited in the rise of Lutheran Protestantism, but, as it turned out, only half of the German people became Protestants, and these were divided between Lutheranism and Calvinism, while the other half remained Catholic. Protracted religio-civil wars ended in the seventeenth century with failure of the emperor to build a German national state and with success of German princes in establishing the practical independence of their three hundred and more states, each with its own economy and each with the religion prescribed by its ruler. Well into the nineteenth century, Germany as a whole was characterized, not by nationalism, but by provincialism of its princes, cosmopolitanism of its intellectuals, and localism of the masses.

In Italy, there was a common religion as well as a common vernacular literature, but the strong tradition of separate city-states and duchies militated against union of the peninsula in a national state, with a national economy; and so too did the papacy, which, fearful of subjection to a national regime, sought to maintain a balance of power, even by favoring foreign intervention of Germans, French, or Spaniards. In both France and Spain, there were communities of literature and religion and forms of national monarchy, but real nationalism was impeded by imperial enterprises, provincial feeling, and local tariffs.

By the seventeenth and early eighteenth centuries, national patriotism was developed more generally and more acutely in England than in any other country—more so than in France or Spain or Sweden, and much more so than in Italy or Germany or eastern Europe. Indeed, we may affirm that modern nationalism, as we know it today, had its original seat in England.[1] Here all four factors which were operating to quicken and exalt national consciousness in western Europe were particularly operative, and all operated together. The distinctive English language was spoken throughout England and the Lowlands of Scotland and it followed the conquests of English Kings into Wales and Ireland. In the 1360's King Edward III prescribed the use of English, instead of Latin or French, in the law courts of England, and simultaneously Chaucer inaugurated the popular English literature which was continued by *Piers Plowman*, Sir Thomas Malory, Cranmer's Book of Common Prayer, and the Elizabethan poets and playwrights.

Medieval English monarchs had been as much French as English and had made protracted efforts to exercise dominion over France. However, their eventual failure in the Hundred Years' War confined their rule to Britain, thereby giving England a truly national monarchy; and under the Tudor sovereigns of the sixteenth century it was a strong and very patriotic national monarchy.

Henry VII reduced the nobility to obedience, and promoted national economy: national shipping and exploration, national industry and mercantilism. Henry VIII had a statute enacted decreeing that "this Realm of England is an Empire," meaning, as Blackstone later said, that "our King is equally sovereign and independent within these his dominions as any Emperor is in his Empire." And, as everybody knows, Henry VIII separated the Anglican Church from Rome, and his daughter Elizabeth made it a definitely Protestant adjunct to the national state. Elizabeth herself was scarcely a devout Christian of any sort, but she was an astute, as well as convinced, patriot, and by playing the role of Protestant champion against Philip II and Catholic Spain she assured the independence and commercial profit of England.

[1] This point is well developed by Hans Kohn in his *Idea of Nationalism, a Study of Its Origins and Background* (1943), ch. IV, pp. 155–183.

In the seventeenth century, it is true, England was torn by protracted civil strife. Absolutist monarchy as practiced by the Stuart kings was opposed by supporters of parliamentary government, and radical Protestant groups—the Puritans—aspiring "to reform the Reformation," assailed the episcopal organization and "superstitious" observances of the Anglican Church as being only a degree less wicked than those of the Roman Church. In the course of the strife, one king was beheaded and another dethroned and forced into exile, and midway in the century, under Cromwell's Puritan dictatorship, Anglicanism was temporarily suppressed in favor of Presbyterianism or Congregationalism.

Yet both sides to the conflict were thoroughly imbued with English patriotism. If Royal England was an "Empire," Puritan England was a "Commonwealth." And in pursuing economic nationalism and fostering overseas colonial settlement, Cromwell vied with the Stuarts. The latter gave their names or titles to English America in Jamestown, Carolina, Maryland, and New York. Cromwell enacted nationalist navigation laws and waged trade war with the Dutch, activities which the restored Stuart, Charles II, continued. Moreover, just as Shakespeare, with his Catholic background, had extolled England in majestic verse in the days of Elizabeth and James I, so in Cromwell's time the Puritan Milton penned sumptuous prose in England's praise.

Wrote Milton, in the *Areopagitica*, with some patriotic exaggeration: "Lords and commons of England! consider what nation it is whereof ye are, and whereof ye are the governors: a nation not slow and dull, but of a quick, ingenious, and piercing spirit; acute to invent, subtile and sinewy to discourse, not beneath the reach of any point the highest that humanity can soar to. Therefore the studies of learning in her deepest sciences have been so ancient, and so eminent among us, that writers of good antiquity and able judgment have been persuaded, that even the school of Pythagoras, and the Persian wisdom, took beginning from the old philosophy of this island. And that wise and civil Roman, Julius Agricola, who governed once here for Caesar, preferred the natural wits of Britain before the laboured studies of the French. . . . Now once again by all concurrence of signs . . . God is decreeing to begin some new and great period. . . . What does he then but reveal himself to his servants, and as his manner is, first to his Englishmen?"

So, Englishmen, at least God-fearing Puritan Englishmen, are God's "chosen people" in modern times, as the Israelites were of yore. Cromwell held the same faith. "The soil of Great Britain," he declared, "is furnished . . . with the best People in the World. . . . And in this People you have, what is still more precious, a People that are to God 'as the apple of His eye'; . . . a People under His safety and protection, a people calling upon the Name of the Lord, which the Heathen do not; a People knowing God; and a People fearing God. And you have of this no parallel; no, not in all the world! . . . God 'hath done things wonderful amongst us . . . terrible things in righteousness.' " Such "righteousness" Cromwell himself served by slaughtering Irish Papists for the sake of British political and religious unity and by fighting Dutch fellow Protestants for British commercial advantage.

The idea of being a "chosen people" has not only been expressed by such Puritan Englishmen as Milton and Cromwell. It has found deep lodgment among their countrymen and among overseas British emigrants. It has been adopted and exemplified by numerous other peoples, most conspicuously today by Dutch Boers of South Africa who combine a rugged Old-Testament Christianity with a rabid nationalism. We may add that many a church in Spain still bears a Latin inscription which reads in translation: "God hath not dealt so with any other nation."

In England the seventeenth-century conflict between king and Parliament was settled toward the close of the century in favor of the latter. Henceforth the king was a figurehead, a kind of animated banner. But this did not lessen English patriotism or stay the progress of English nationalism. Autocratic monarchy had already accomplished its nationalizing function in England. Popular loyalty to a king had passed into loyalty to his law, and now it passed definitely into loyalty to the national state. The political philosophy of John

Locke, the Whig, and that of Lord Bolingbroke, the Tory, might differ in emphasis and detail, but not in glorification of the English nation and the "British Constitution."

England pioneered in the new popular nationalism. The American Revolution would mark its advent among British colonists in the New World, and the French Revolution would introduce it, with quasi-religious zeal, to the European Continent.

CHAPTER V

Making Nationalism a Religion in Revolutionary France

1. Deist and Classical Setting

The great French Revolution in the last decade of the eighteenth century is a bulking landmark in the history of modern nationalism. It marks not only the transit of nationalism from England to the European Continent, but its emergence in democratic and essentially religious form. The way for this was paved during the preceding century and a half by two intellectual developments in western Europe. One was the Enlightenment; the other was Pietism.

The Enlightenment involved a rationalistic skepticism concerning "revealed" or "supernatural" religion, particularly Christianity. It represented a reaction against the theological disputes and religious fanaticism of the era of the Reformation. It also reflected an admiration for what was heard from afar of non-Christian peoples and religions, of naked savages in America who lived in natural virtue and happiness without clergymen or creeds, and of highly cultured natives of China and India who lived philosophically without benefit of Christianity. But most important in prompting rationalist skepticism was the influence of contemporary discoveries and speculations in natural science. For, if the universe was simply a huge machine, functioning in accordance with natural law, what place was left in it for a supernatural religion? Was not religion itself, like physics, merely natural? Could not true religion be discovered, like Newton's law of gravitation, by human reason without recourse to "revelation" or "authority"?

One of the earliest champions of this view was an English nobleman, Baron Herbert of Cherbury. In two treatises—*On Truth as it is distinguished from Revelation,* printed in 1624 and *On Religion of the Heathen,* published posthumously in 1663—he maintained that "natural religion," consisting of belief in God, virtue, and immortality, is all that reason and common sense dictate, and that religious revelations are inventions of priests. Herbert was followed by Thomas Hobbes, materialist and political philosopher, who argued for the omnipotence of the secular state; and he in turn by Lord Bolingbroke, the Tory politician of the early eighteenth century, who used his literary talents to attack "traditional Christianity" and to exalt national patriotism.[1] Bolingbroke collaborated in writing the anthem:

> "Rule, Britannia, rule the waves;
> Britons never will be slaves."

According to these English skeptics, there was a God but he was merely the first cause of natural law, the original giver of reason, natural rights, and an impulse to progress. He had once, at the beginning, acted in the grand manner by starting things, but ever afterward he was fated to be a helpless supernumerary of the physical universe, enchained by the natural laws which he had decreed for human beings and for the stars, and incapable of working miracles or heeding prayers. To this "natural" religion, Englishmen gave the name of "Deism," and Englishmen provided a kind of church for it in the Freemasonry they founded in the 1710's.

From England, Deism, with attendant Freemasonry, was exported to the Continent, and particularly in France it found in Voltaire a brilliant and voluminous advocate, and became the veritable religion of a large section of the upper and middle classes. Here, a few went further and, like Holbach, turned Atheist, contending that there is no God at all, not even a God of Nature, and inditing abusive prop-

[1] I have discussed Bolingbroke, a bit irreverently, in "The Philosopher Turned Patriot," *Essays in Intellectual History Dedicated to James Harvey Robinson* (1929).

aganda under such titles as *Christianity Unveiled*, and *Priests Unmasked*.

In general, the Deistic Enlightenment did contribute to an access of tolerance and reforming spirit in Western Christendom. Religious persecution (except of Jesuits) declined, and humanitarian movements were set in motion to reform prisons and legal practices, to emancipate Jews and Negroes, to promote international peace; in a word, to "rationalize" human society. Occasionally some persons, envisioning Deism as the future world religion, even disclaimed any national patriotism. The German Lessing, for instance, a good Deist, confessed that "love of country is at best but an heroic vice which I am quite content to be without." Thomas Paine, an even more voluble Deist, boasted that "the world is my country: mankind are my brothers."

Nevertheless, it is an arresting fact that the era of the Enlightenment, which witnessed among the classes the growth of skepticism about Christianity, witnessed also a substitute exaltation—a sanctification, as it were—of the secular state, especially of the national state. Bolingbroke wanted a Church of England, though it must not "involve anything superstitious or theological," or lay claim to any independence of the national state, which should "direct the public and private influence of the clergy in a strict conformity to the letter and spirit of the British Constitution, the servants of which in a much truer sense they are than what they affect sometimes to call themselves, the ambassadors of God to other men." Outstanding patriots, according to Bolingbroke, should be the saints of the State Church —an admonition since largely realized in Westminster Abbey.

Or, as a famed French Deist and patriot, the ex-Abbé Raynal, later declared: "The State is not made for religion: religion is made for the state. . . . The State is supreme in all things. Any distinction between temporal power and spiritual power is a palpable absurdity. . . ."

Classical education, in which men of the Enlightenment were reared, fed the notion that patriotism is a noble virtue, that its proper object is one's country and state, and that its fruits are love of liberty and hatred of tyranny. To be sure, the patriotism which ancient Greeks and Romans had extolled was not national patriotism. In the case of the Greeks it was urban patriotism; in that of the Romans it was first urban and then imperial.

But men of the seventeenth and eighteenth centuries did not hesitate to apply it to their respective nations. Plutarch's *Lives* were extremely influential; they ran through many editions in the original Greek and more in vernacular translation; a French commentary on them, published in 1664, described the patriotic chant of the Spartans in manner suggestive of the *Marseillaise* of a later day. D'Aguesseau's panegyric on the death of Louis XIV in 1715 was replete with classical reference and redolent of antique patriotism. Alfieri, the foremost Italian dramatist of the eighteenth century, dwelt on the classical theme of popular liberty in arms against the tyrant. Frederick the Great of Prussia wrote, albeit in French, a book on patriotism in style and spirit that might be Athenian, or, more likely, Spartan. The fathers of American independence rolled classic patriotic phrases on their tongues, and the histrionic "Give me liberty or give me death" of a Patrick Henry echoed Brutus's *Sic semper tyrannis,* which was duly adopted as the motto of revolutionary Virginia.

When the French Revolution came, every leader in it was steeped in the classics, and most of them in Deism. The Girondists, for example —Brissot, Vergniaud, the Rolands, *et al.*—stood valiantly for antique republican virtue and only the guillotine stilled their classical oratory. The Hébert-Chaumette group were atheist, it is true, but Robespierre the Deist beheaded them with the guillotine.

2. *Pietist and Proto-Romantic Setting*

The religious skepticism of many European intellectuals was paralleled during the Enlightenment by the Pietist movement among large numbers of people who retained an ardent personal belief in Christianity but generally disregarded any elaborate, reasoned theology. Pietism emphasized emotion and enthusiasm in religion, a mystical "conversion" of the individual from sinner to saint, a lessening if not obliteration of distinction between clergy and laity.

The movement took many forms and was especially notable in Protestant countries. In England—and English America—it was represented by Congregationalists, Baptists, and other "Non-Conformists"; by George Fox, William Penn, and the Quakers; by the Wesleys and the Methodists with their evangelists and "revival meetings" and hymn-singing appeal to the lower classes. In Germany it was preached by Philipp Spener and numerous followers of his among the Lutherans, and also by such sects as the Moravian Brethren and the Mennonites. In Scandinavia, Swedenborg, who acquired fame as a scientist, had "heaven opened to him" in 1710, and from his mystical revelations sprang the Church of the New Jerusalem.

Catholic countries were not untouched by Pietism. It appeared in Flanders and France in puritanical Jansenism, in Spain and France in Quietism. Pascal inclined toward the one; Fénélon, toward the other. Both movements were eventually condemned by the Church. But such action encountered protracted opposition, not alone from those condemned, but from many skeptically inclined intellectuals, who increased the adverse criticism of ecclesiastical authority, particularly of the papacy.

Pietism was in itself, of course, a strictly religious affair, and probably at the outset none of its various leaders was consciously aware of any such force as nationalism. Nevertheless, it prepared an intellectual and spiritual *milieu* favorable to the development of nationalism. Its emphasis on emotion, on variety and individuality, on popular schooling, could readily be applied to nationality, and prominent Pietists of the eighteenth century did so. "God has pointed out to every people," declared Schleiermacher, "its particular mission on earth and has breathed into it its particular spirit, in order that in this way He may be glorified by each one through its particular mode."[1]

Pietism, too, was intertwined with, and in measure a phase of, the "proto-romanticism" which represented in art and mood a reaction

[1] The relationship between Pietism and nationalism is admirably treated by Koppel S. Pinson in an article in *Christendom*, vol. I, pp. 266–280 (Winter, 1936). He also has a monograph on the subject.

against the "artificiality" and "unnaturalness" of classicism. This proto-romanticism stressed individuality (personal and national), and the importance of common scenes and common people. It was a "back-to-nature" movement. It found "natural beauty," not in classical Rome or Greece, but in the Alps, in English lakes and Scottish highlands, in fiords of Norway and trackless forests of America, in simple landscapes, in tombs and weeping willows. It extolled "natural man": the Chinese sage and the noble savage of America, the common man with natural virtue untrammeled by superstition or artificial civilization. It stirred "natural feeling," which could easily be transfused into national feeling, as was done by the *Sturm und Drang* literary movement in Germany, by the English Lake poets, by Robert Burns in Scotland, by Jean Jacques Rousseau.

Rousseau is well known, of course, as a romantic, as a philosopher of political democracy, and as an educational reformer. He should also be known as a champion of nationalism. In 1772, at the request of a Polish nobleman, he wrote an essay advising how a people, in this case the Poles, might intensify their national patriotism. After relating how Moses welded the Jews "into a nation" by means of special laws and rites, Rousseau affirms that "it is the national institutions which form the genius, the character, the tastes, and the customs of a people . . . and which inspire the ardent love of country." As devices for quickening this national patriotism, he mentions the award of special honors to meritorious citizens, the revival of national customs, the holding of national games, the presentation of national plays, and the observance of holidays which should "breathe patriotism." Most important of such devices would be national schooling: "a child in opening its eyes ought to see *la patrie*" and until death ought to see no other; all should be educated in "the love of country, that is to say, in the love of liberty and the laws." And only second to national education should be a national militia; "each citizen ought to be a soldier by duty."

Rousseau died eleven years before the French Revolution began, but on the leaders and course of the Revolution his ideas and preachments had enormous influence. Not least among these was nationalism.

3. From American Revolution to French National Assembly

Both Pietism and the Enlightenment, both romanticism and classicism, were practically exemplified as supports of nationalism by the revolutionary movement in America from 1775 to 1789.[1] Here was cooperation between evangelical Pietists of New England and such Deists as Franklin and Jefferson, and among "enlightened" Anglicans like Washington, Catholics like the Carrolls of Maryland, and a Jew like Haym Salomon. Here was a Declaration of Independence, appealing to natural law and affirming natural rights. Here was an emerging national union, with one of the earliest written constitutions, abolishing monarchy and aristocracy, separating church from state, and guaranteeing individual liberty through Bill of Rights and Supreme Court.

Here, obviously, along with "republican virtue" was the wisdom of simple "natural men."

"The United States of America" was a somewhat pretentious title for a nation which in 1789 was relatively insignificant in population, industry, and culture. But the new nation excited a curiosity and had an influence in Europe, and particularly in France, out of all proportion to its size and strength. French alliance and armed aid had been decisive in establishing its independence. Thousands of French soldiers and marines had fought in it side by side with Americans. Millions of French francs had been expended for it. Indeed, this expenditure was the immediate cause of the French Revolution.

By 1789 French public finance was in chaos. For a century expenditure had been tremendous on a succession of major wars: War of the League of Augsburg (1689–1697), War of the Spanish Succession (1701–1713), War of the Polish Succession (1733–1735), War of the Austrian Succession (1740–1748), Seven Years' War (1756–1763), and, latest, War of American Independence (1778–1783). Parallel expenditure—and indebtedness—had been mounting for court and sinecures as well as for an extremely complex administration. Simul-

[1] For a thoughtful and well written account of the revolutionary movement on both sides of the Atlantic, see Robert R. Palmer, *The Age of the Democratic Revolution, 1760–1800* (1959).

taneously, income was grossly abridged by the exemption of "privileged classes"—nobility and clergy—from payment of most taxes. And no real reform was wrought by the indolent Louis XV or the well intentioned but weak Louis XVI. The latter did convene an "Assembly of Notables" in 1787 in the hope of averting bankruptcy by inducing the privileged classes to share the financial burden. It was in vain. The Assembly merely advised the king to call the Estates-General—which had had no meeting for a hundred and seventy-five years!

The royal summons was addressed, in the plural, to "my peoples," and elections were held in medieval style, indirectly and by class. The clergy (First Estate) and the nobility (Second Estate) chose 300 representatives each, and, by special permission of the king, the common people (Third Estate) elected 600. Each electoral unit was invited to prepare a *cahier*, or "grievance list"; and study of the cahiers shows that, in general, national spirit was most marked in and around Paris and less so as one approached outlying provinces of Brittany, Picardy, Alsace, Provence, and Navarre.[1]

The Estates-General met at Versailles in May 1789, and issue was speedily joined on the manner of voting. The old custom of voting separately by Estate was favored by clergy and nobility and the king, but the Third Estate, claiming that it represented the nation at large, defied custom, proclaimed itself a "National Assembly," and invited the other Estates to merge with it, in which all members would vote as individuals and not by class. This was revolution, but after some hesitation the king, toward the close of June, 1789, accepted it and authorized the transformation of the Estates-General into the National Assembly.

We shall not recount here any detailed story of Revolutionary

---

[1] See Beatrice Hyslop, *French Nationalism in the General Cahiers of 1789*, and Robert R. Palmer, "The National Idea in France Before the Revolution," *Journal of History of Ideas*, I, 95–111 (1940). For special light on various nationalist aspects of the Revolution, one might consult Glyndon Van Deusen's *Sieyès;* James M. Eagan's *Robespierre;* Georgia Robison Beale's *Revellière-lépeaux;* Leo Gershoy's "Barère," *Political Science Quarterly*, XLII, 419–30; and Huntley Dupré's *Carnot, Republican Patriot*.

France during the momentous decade from 1789 to 1799. We shall confine ourselves rather to noting major nationalistic developments. The adoption of the title, "National Assembly," was one of the first, and it was soon followed by the Assembly's promulgation of the "Declaration of the Rights of Man and of the Citizen," the third item of which read: "The principle of all sovereignty resides essentially in the nation; no body nor individual may exercise any authority which does not proceed directly from the nation."

Then ensued, beginning in August, 1789, a nationalistic leveling process. There was abolition of feudal survivals, of serfdom, of class privileges, of the hereditary judiciary, of the university corporations, of the guilds. There was recruiting of "national guards," supplementary to the royal army. There was confiscation of church property with the avowed purpose of rescuing the nation from bankruptcy, and the according of full toleration to Protestants and Jews. Still further to ensure national equality and unity, there was a blotting out of provincial boundaries and provincial "rights," and substitution of uniform administrative districts, the *départements*.

Protests against the nationalizing of the historic provinces of France were met by "federation" demonstrations organized by national guardsmen and other patriots. In November, 1789, some 12,000 townsmen and peasants, assembled at Etoile on the Rhone, from the provinces of Languedoc and Dauphiné, solemnly affirmed that "abjuring every distinction of our provinces, offering our arms and our wealth to *la patrie* for support of the laws which come from the National Assembly, we swear to give all possible succor to each other to fulfill these duties and to fly to the help of our brothers of Paris or of any town of France which may be in danger in the cause of liberty." In January, 1790, National Guardsmen of Anjou and Brittany met and took a similar oath, while the city of Dijon called upon Burgundy to demonstrate in like manner with Lyons and Franche-Comté. In May a big federation meeting was held at Lyons, and in June, at the request of the mayor and commune of Paris, the National Assembly convoked a General Federation. The date selected was the first anniversary of the mob destruction of that symbol of royal absolutism, the Bastille.

So, on July 14, 1790, a vast nationalist fete was held on the Champs de Mars. In attendance were the king and queen, 50,000 delegates from all parts of France, 14,000 national guardsmen, 160,000 others seated and 150,000 standing. Bishop Talleyrand celebrated Mass, assisted by two hundred priests. Twelve hundred musicians played. Forty cannons were fired. Everybody took the federation oath. On that day representatives of Celtic Brittany, half-Flemish Picardy, half-Spanish Roussillon, almost wholly German Alsace and Italian Corsica swore brotherhood—*fraternité*—with the French. No wonder that July 14 became the country's national holiday.

On the eve of the grand fete on the Champs de Mars, a group of inhabitants of the papal territory of Avignon petitioned the National Assembly for annexation to France. Avignon had belonged to the papacy since the fourteenth century, but in July, 1791, despite vigorous papal protests, the National Assembly sent French troops into the city and, following a perfunctory favorable plebiscite, annexed it. Thus was introduced the new and revolutionary principle of "national self-determination," the principle that people have a right not only of self-government but of transferring themselves from one sovereignty to another. A natural result of the application of the principle in the case of Avignon was alarm of such neighboring powers as Austria, Sardinia, and Britain concerning what the French revolutionaries might do in the Netherlands and Savoy. The alarm proved well founded, as nationalist France went on in the 1790's to annex the Belgian Netherlands, Savoy and Nice, and the Rhineland, and to set up satellite regimes in the Dutch Netherlands, in Switzerland, and all over Italy.

Nationalist propaganda became a fine art with the French revolutionaries. It was exercised by Masonic lodges, by clubs like the Jacobin and Cordelier, by the federations and national guards, by the local communes (especially that of Paris), and, above all, by a flood of newspapers and pamphlets so cheap and so demagogic as to appeal to the half-educated masses even more than to intellectuals. To the same end, legislation was enacted imposing on all French citizens the "central or national language" (that is, French) and penalizing the use of "patois" (Breton, Flemish, Provençal, Basque, and so on).

Before the Revolution, schooling in most countries had been private and voluntary, a privilege of a minority, and it had inculcated religion and morality. In the Constitution which the National Assembly completed in 1791 was a clause foreshadowing different, nationalist education. "There shall be created and organized," it read, "a system of public instruction common to all the citizens and gratuitous in respect to those subjects which are indispensable to all men. Schools of various grades shall be supplied according to need over the entire kingdom. Commemorative days shall be designated for the purpose of preserving the memory of the French Revolution, of developing the spirit of fraternity among all citizens, and of attaching them to the Constitution, to *la patrie*, and its laws." In other words, schooling was henceforth to be public and free, a right of everybody, and definitely nationalist. Just such a plan was drafted by a Committee under Talleyrand's chairmanship and was submitted to the National Assembly in September 1791.

As the National Assembly was then on the point of putting into effect the limited constitutional monarchy it had devised, it passed on the educational plan to the succeeding Legislative Assembly. This body appointed a new committee, headed by the philosopher Condorcet, who reported an amended and even more nationalist plan. Money was lacking for it, however. Foreign war was beginning, and it seemed less needful at the moment to put the nation in school than to put it in arms.

Compulsory national education remained an ideal, but its realization was deferred. Compulsory army service became both an ideal and a reality, a crusading aspect of the religion of nationalism which the French Revolution evolved.

4. Religious Emblems and Crusading Zeal

Quasi-religious emblems attended the revolutionary progress of nationalism in France. A national flag—the tricolor—was compounded in 1789 of the red-and-blue of Paris and the white of the Bourbon king. A national holiday was celebrated every year on July 14, anniversary both of the destruction of the Bastille and of the Paris Federation Fete. A national anthem—the rousing *Marseillaise*—was composed by Rouget de Lisle in 1792 and first sung by a band of soldiers from Marseilles marching in Paris for the overthrow of the monarchy. Other emblems cropped up: liberty caps, Phrygian caps, Roman fasces, trees of liberty, long-pants uniforms (*sans-culottes*) for patriots, altars to the fatherland.

The Declaration of the Rights of Man and of the Citizen was treated as a national catechism, and profession of faith in it was prescribed by the Constitution of 1791. Anyone refusing to swear to it was cut off from the community by civil excommunication; and foreigners who swore loyalty to it were admitted to the ranks of the faithful and enrolled as in a communion of saints. At the first session of the Legislative Assembly, in the autumn of 1791, "twelve old men went in procession to seek the Book of the Constitution. They came back, having at their head the archivist Camus, who, holding up the book with his two hands and resting it on his breast, carried with slow and measured tread the new Blessed Sacrament of the French. All the deputies stood up and bared their heads. Camus, with meditative mien, kept his eyes lowered."[1] The same Assembly decreed in June, 1792, that "in all the communes an altar to the fatherland shall be raised and on it shall be written the Declaration of Rights, with the inscription: 'The citizen is born, lives, and dies for *la patrie.*'" Two years earlier, at Strasbourg, a rite of "civic baptism" was introduced jointly by a priest, a minister, and a rabbi. "Civic marriages" and "civic funerals" came later, and likewise the many, many graves of soldier citizens with the epitaph, *Mort pour la patrie*—"Dead for the fatherland"!

At first an attempt was made to reconcile the new religion of nationalism with the traditional Christian religion of France—at the expense of the latter. The confiscation of church property for financial benefit of the state was theoretically compensated, and the

[1] A. Mathiez, *Les origines des cultes révolutionaires* (1904), p. 27.

Church shackled to the national state, by the Civil Constitution of the Clergy which went into effect in 1791. According to the Civil Constitution, priests and bishops were to be elected by the people, paid by the state, and only nominally associated with the pope, and they were to take an oath of allegiance to the new arrangement.

This kind of reconciliation failed, however. Pope Pius VI, who had already protested against the confiscation of church property, the suppression of monasteries, and the seizure of Avignon, condemned the Civil Constitution and forbade the French clergy to take the required oath. Those who did take the oath—the "juring" clergy—were excommunicated. Such as refused—the "nonjuring" clergy—were deprived of their salaries and threatened with imprisonment. Thus the Catholic Church in France was split in twain, and laid open for assault by the anti-Christian revolutionaries. The king, who had opposed the Civil Constitution and had signed it only under duress, tried in vain to escape his virtual imprisonment in Paris. He was brought back, and not much more than a year later, amidst foreign war and Parisian rioting, he was replaced by the radically revolutionary Republic and was put to death.

Now the nonjuring clergy could expect no mercy: they were guillotined or they fled abroad. Even the juring clergy were now suspect. In October, 1793, to discourage observance of the Christian Sunday, the Republican National Convention decreed a new calendar with the tenth day in each month being a day of rest, and five days at the end of the year being national festivals.

In November 1793 Marie-Joseph de Chénier, the poet, proposed to the Convention the formal establishment of nationalism as the state religion. "Wrest," he said, "the sons of the Republic from the yoke of theocracy which still weighs upon them. . . . Devoid of prejudices and worthy to represent the French nation, you will know how to found, on the debris of the dethroned superstitions, the only universal religion which has neither sects nor mysteries, of which the only dogma is equality, of which our lawmakers are the preachers, of which the magistrates are the pontiffs, and in which the human family burns its incense only at the altar of *la patrie*—common mother and divinity." Two days later the Catholic Bishop of Paris announced to the Convention his apostasy from Christianity, explaining that "there should no longer be any public worship other than that of liberty and holy equality." Three days more, and the worship of Reason was inaugurated, with great fanfare, in the cathedral of Notre Dame.

Reason proved too abstract, too atheistic, perhaps too remote from current events in revolutionary France, to obtain permanent national adoration. Robespierre certainly objected to it, and under his influence it was soon succeeded by a deistic cult of the Supreme Being. Later, after Robespierre's downfall and the installation of the Directory, a kind of ceremonial "ethical culture" was made the official religion under the awesome title of "Theophilanthropy." But whatever vitality there was in any or all of these varieties and vagaries of religious experimentation is attributable to their infusion with the religion of nationalism.

Nor can one understand the crusading zeal with which foreign war was waged by French revolutionaries without perceiving a main motivation in religious nationalism. Doubtless the first declaration of war, in April, 1792, was occasioned by the threatening attitude of the Austrian Emperor and his henchman, the King of Prussia. But it was accompanied by a long novel pronunciamento, at once idealistic and propagandist: "that the French nation, faithful to the principles consecrated by its constitution 'not to undertake any war with a view to conquest nor ever to employ its forces against the liberty of any people,' only takes up arms for the maintenance of its liberty and independence; that the war which it is forced to prosecute is not a war of nation against nation . . . ; that the French nation never confuses its brethren with its real enemies; that it will neglect nothing which may reduce the curse of war, spare and preserve property, and cause all the unhappiness inseparable from war to fall alone upon those who have conspired against its liberty; that it adopts in advance all foreigners, who, abjuring the cause of its enemies, shall range themselves under its banners and consecrate their efforts to the defense of liberty; and that it will promote by all means in its power their settling in France. . . ."

Alas, no appreciable number of foreigners (except a minority in the Belgian Netherlands) abjured the cause of Austrian emperor and Prussian king. Armies of these sovereigns invaded France and were only halted in September, 1792, at Valmy. This was occasion for the September massacres at Paris, for the convocation of the Republican National Convention, and, two months later, for the issuance of a new and quite different pronunciamento concerning the war. "The French nation declares," we are now told, "that it will treat as enemies every people who, refusing liberty and equality or renouncing them, may wish to maintain, recall, or treat with the prince and the privileged classes; on the other hand, it engages not to subscribe to any treaty and not to lay down its arms until the sovereignty and independence of the peoples whose territory the troops of the Republic shall have entered shall be established, and until the people shall have adopted the principles of equality and founded a free and democratic government."

French armies were presently ensuring the incorporation of Savoy and Nice and of the Belgian Netherlands in revolutionary France, while against them Austria and Prussia were being joined by Sardinia, Great Britain, the Dutch Netherlands, and Spain. Simultaneously, revolts of conservatives and Catholics broke out within France, particularly at Lyons and in La Vendée and Brittany. The Revolutionaries replied with the Reign of Terror, with conscription, with totalitarian war. A decree of August, 1793, called for military service of all Frenchmen between the ages of eighteen and twenty-five, with the added instruction: "The young men shall go to battle; the married men shall forge arms and transport provisions; the women shall make tents and clothing and shall serve in the hospitals; the old people shall betake themselves to the public places in order to arouse the courage of the warriors and to preach hatred of kings and unity of the Republic."

Four months later a young warrior, a certain François Xavier Joliclerc, was writing his mother: "When the country calls us for its defense, we ought to hasten to it as I would hasten to a good meal. Our life, our goods, our talents do not belong to us. All such belong to the nation, to *la patrie*. . . . Principles of love of country, love of liberty, love of the Republic are not only engraved on my heart; they are enshrined there, and there they will remain as long as it will please the Supreme Being to keep a breath of life in me."

An essentially religious enthusiasm of young Joliclerc's sort must have animated a multitude of his fellows. Thanks to it, as well as to the ferocious determination of the Republican regime, the organizing genius of its military chief, Carnot, and the ability of revolutionary generals in the field, domestic revolt was crushed and foreign enemy coalitions were dissolved. Prussia, Sardinia, the Dutch Netherlands, and Spain owned defeat and made peace in 1795, Austria in 1797, Great Britain in 1801. Nationalist France obtained in five years, against seemingly overwhelming odds, the "natural frontiers" which the France of Louis XIV had failed to get in seventy years, and a string of satellite states besides. Nationalist France also produced Napoleon Bonaparte.

CHAPTER VI

Advance of Nationalism in Europe from Napoleon I to Napoleon III
1800–1870

1. Under the First Napoleon

Napoleon Bonaparte was at least a stepson of the French Revolution. Beginning as a Corsican patriot, he grew up to combine French revolutionary nationalism with vaulting personal ambition. During his amazing career, from the first Italian campaign in 1796 to the last engagement at Waterloo in 1815, in turn career general, Consul of the Republic, and Emperor of the French, he personified revolutionary and nationalist principles. He maintained for the French the principle, if not the practice, of national democratic sovereignty, of equality and fraternity if not of liberty. He kept the national tricolor flag, and the "Marseillaise" as the national anthem. He stirred his armies with patriotic speeches, impressed the public with patriotic ritual, founded the patriotic Legion of Honor. He gave permanency to leveling social reforms of the Revolution by incorporating them in the monumental *Code Napoléon.*

He actually inaugurated what such revolutionaries as Talleyrand and Condorcet had proposed—the putting of the nation in state schools. He continued and developed to the full the putting of the nation (and all possible allies) in arms.

Bonaparte eased the conflict between the Catholic religion and that of French nationalism by negotiating a concordat with the

59

papacy,[1] though he subsequently restricted the freedom of the Church and imprisoned the pope. His own religion was fundamentally egotist and nationalist.

In 1792, when the revolutionary wars began, there had been relatively slight nationalist spirit among the masses on the European Continent outside of France. But as the wars went on, and especially under Napoleon, it was aroused and spread by several means. First, extensive areas were incorporated into France—the Belgian Netherlands, the German Rhineland, the Italian districts of Savoy and Nice—and for twenty years they shared intimately in its revolutionary heritage. Secondly, a string of dependent and allied territories came under French tutelage—the Italian peninsula, the Dutch Netherlands, nearly half of Germany (the "Confederation of the Rhine"), Denmark, Poland (the "Grand Duchy of Warsaw"), the "Illyrian provinces" (a strip of what is now Yugoslavia along the Adriatic), and (briefly) Spain and Portugal. Even in Sweden a Napoleonic Marshal, Bernadotte, was elected heir to the throne. Thirdly, peoples near France, and as far away from it as Austria and Russia, saw repeatedly the marching and camping of French armies and must have noted the patriotic ceremonies attending them. In time a goodly number of foreign troops—German, Italian, Polish, for instance— were intermixed, as allies, with Napoleon's nationalist French forces.

Most important for the spread of nationalism was the patriotic reaction on the part of foreign writers, statesmen, and eventually peoples, against the militancy of France, the Revolution, and Napoleon. This reaction began, as one might expect, in England, where it was sparked as early as 1790 by Edmund Burke's famous attack on the French Revolution and defense of Britain's "traditional" nationalism.[2] Burke had an enormous influence, not only in England but on the Continent, with monarchs, aristocrats, and churchmen. He campaigned vociferously for war with revolutionary France, and, from 1793 past his death four years later and on until 1815, Great

[1] Nationalistic background and features of the Concordat have been presented in an excellent monograph by Henry H. Walsh (1933).

[2] I have dealt with the "traditional" nationalism of Burke, Bonald, and Schlegel in *The Historical Evolution of Modern Nationalism,* pp. 84–119.

Britain was the center and mainstay of every coalition of European powers arrayed against Revolutionary and Napoleonic France. To its earlier national heroes and demigods, Britain now added the younger Pitt, Nelson, and Wellington, while on the Continent it was the constant champion of "oppressed peoples."

To the traditional nationalism of Burke's sort was drawn, moreover, a number of antirevolutionary French conservatives. One of these, the Vicomte de Bonald, wrote from exile in 1796 a glowing tribute to French language, religion, history, and "character." Five years later the romantic Chateaubriand issued a celebrated new apologia for Catholic Christianity, making claim not for its truth, but for its beauty, for its ennobling of French national patriotism, for its being basic to modern revolutionary principles of "liberty, equality, fraternity." If Frenchmen were divided by the Revolution, "Right" could eventually vie with "Left," and surpass it, in nationalist devotion.

Exponents of *German* nationalism grew numerous and noisy. Johann Gottlieb Fichte, while professor of philosophy at Jena in the 1790's had been a "fellow traveler" with the French revolutionaries, acclaiming their achievements and indoctrinating his university students with the principles of "liberty, equality, and fraternity." The Prussian defeat at Jena in 1806 changed Fichte. Henceforth he was a bitter foe of Napoleon and the French and a strenuous advocate of German unity. His ultrapatriotic *Addresses to the German Nation* were followed by his appointment to a chair in the newly founded University of Berlin. Meanwhile in a pamphlet entitled "The German Republic," he romantically described the worship he foresaw in the "national church" of the future: "On Sunday morning . . . when all parishioners have arrived, the church doors are thrown open and amid soft music the congregation enters. . . . When all are seated the great curtains at the altar are drawn aside, revealing the cannon, muskets, and other weapons which constitute the parish armory. For every German youth from his twentieth birthday to his death is a soldier. Then there appears before the congregation the justice of the peace, who unfurls the flag. . . ." It was a fitting end to Fichte that he died of cholera in 1814 while nursing soldiers in the War of Liberation, a martyr to the cause of German nationalism.[1]

Both Ernst Arndt, of Protestant peasant stock, and Joseph von Görres, of a well-to-do Catholic family in Coblenz, were at first, like Fichte, enthusiastic supporters of the French Revolution. Both, however, turned against Napoleon, Arndt being distressed by observing the war-ruined castles on the Rhine, and Görres becoming reconverted to Catholicism and associating with it a veneration for historic Germany of the Middle Ages. Both Görres and Arndt devoted great talents to nationalist journalism and propaganda.[2]

Friedrich Schleiermacher, the Pietist, after extolling the individuality of persons and nations, was transformed by the Prussian defeat at Jena into an almost fanatical patriot. He preached nationalist sermons. He urged a merging of Lutherans and Calvinists in a national church for Germany. There was also the nationalistic Friedrich Jahn—"Vater" Jahn—preacher, pedagogue, and gymnast, a rugged, eccentric precursor of "Boy Scouts" and "Davy Crocketts."[3]

German statesmen, too, fostered nationalism as a weapon against Napoleonic imperialism. To arouse national spirit in German Austria, the Habsburg emperor established a propaganda bureau and entrusted it to the romantic Friedrich von Schlegel.[4] In Prussia, following the disaster at Jena, Baron vom Stein was instrumental in abolishing serfdom and preparing for the War of Liberation, while Wilhelm von Humboldt, as minister of public instruction, founded the University of Berlin and made it a cultural center of German nationalism. Both Stein and Humboldt utilized the propagandist activities of the galaxy of patriots here mentioned—Fichte, Arndt, Görres, Schleiermacher, even "Vater" Jahn.

Among *Italians,* Vittorio Alfieri, their leading dramatist, conceived

---

[1] The late H. C. Engelbrecht left a useful study of Fichte's nationalism (1933).

[2] On Arndt's nationalism, see the monograph by Alfred G. Pundt.

[3] Hans Kohn has written on Vater Jahn, *Review of Politics,* XI, 419–432 (1949), and on Arndt, *American Historical Review,* LIV, 787–803 (1949).

[4] See Walter C. Langsam's *Napoleonic Wars and German Nationalism in Austria* (1930).

a strong dislike of the French Revolution while residing during its early stages in Paris, and he reacted violently against the subsequent French invasion of Italy. In 1799 appeared his *Misogallo,* a fierce polemic in prose and verse. Italians, it contended, were far better than Frenchmen; they had a superior language and literature, and better manners; to put a stop to their exploitation by the French, they must unite and be proud, and these ends they could best achieve through cultivation of a common hatred of the French.[1]

There were also Vincenzo Cuoco, historian and educator, who urged the stimulation of Italian national consciousness through a uniform system of public schooling, and Ugo Foscolo, the poet, who eloquently but vainly besought Napoleon to unite and free Italy, and who later, for turning his eloquence against the French, was silenced, and his career ended with exile in England. And curiously enough, it was during the rule of Naples by Napoleon's brother-in-law, Murat, and probably with his connivance, that the secret, revolutionary, and nationalist society of the "Charcoal Burners" (Carbonari) was formed.

Mention might similarly be made of such *Polish* patriots of the era as Thaddeus Kosciusko and Prince Adam Czartoryski, and of the *Greek* patriots Koraes and Rhigas and the Ypsilantis.[2] A particularly striking example of nationalist reaction against Napoleon and the French was furnished by the popular *Spanish* uprising of "eighth of May" (1808). Here Britain furnished direct military aid, and the ensuing Peninsular War proved a major factor in Napoleon's overthrow.[3] And notable among the fighting Spanish patriots was a young colonial from Venezuela, Simón Bolívar, who subsequently won fame as revolutionary "Liberator" of Spanish-American nations.

Then, too, from the burning of Moscow, which climaxed Napo-

[1] For details, see *Alfieri, Forerunner of Italian Nationalism,* by the late Gaudence Megaro (1930).

[2] On Koraes, there is a useful monograph by Stephen G. Chaconas (1941).

[3] See Beatrice F. Hyslop, "French Jacobin Nationalism and Spain," *Nationalism and Internationalism,* ed. by Edward M. Earle (1951); and Edward J. Goodman, "Spanish Nationalism in the Struggle Against Napoleon," *Review of Politics,* XX, 330–346 (1958), and his Columbia dissertation *Nationalism in the Cortes of Cadiz* (1951).

leon's ill-fated invasion of Russia in 1812, the impressionable Tsar Alexander received, he said later, the patriotic "illumination" which moved him to assume leadership of what he regarded as a crusade against the French emperor. The decisive five-day battle at Leipzig in October of the next year has been appropriately dubbed the Battle of the Nations.

2. From Vienna Peace Settlement to the 1830's

The Congress of Vienna (1814–1815) registered the international peace settlement that terminated the Revolutionary and Napoleonic Wars which had ravaged Europe for twenty-three years. Its chief architect was Prince Metternich, who was no nationalist. Indeed he regarded nationalism as subversive of social security and the traditional state system of Europe, as inimical specifically to the polyglot nature of the Habsburg Empire he served, and as dangerous in general to European peace. For what would the triumph of nationalism entail? A series, he foresaw, of ruinous international wars, revolutionary rearrangement of boundaries, and partition of the Empire.

The settlement of 1815 corresponded, in the main, with Metternich's wishes. In the interest of a restored "balance of power," France was allowed to retain its frontiers of 1792 (including Alsace, but not Savoy or Nice), while, to hold France in check, the Rhineland and Westphalia were added to Prussia, and Belgium to the Dutch Netherlands. The nonnational Austrian Empire was bolstered and extended: it annexed outright two major Italian states (Venetia and Lombardy) and dominated the others into which the peninsula was redivided; and it secured hegemony over the several German states. Metternich thought in European, not in nationalist, terms. He was one of a dwindling number of cosmopolitan statesmen in Europe.

Nationalist aspirations were voiced, it is true, at Vienna, particularly by the emotional and ambitious Tsar Alexander, and by such persons in his entourage as Prince Czartoryski, the Polish patriot, and Stein and Humboldt, the Prussian patriots. But their hopes were very imperfectly realized. Only a part of Poland was resuscitated as a constitutional monarchy with the tsar as king. And although a German Confederation was formed, it was a loose one of princes, headed by the Austrian emperor, rather than a compact one of the German nationality.[1]

Nevertheless, even while the Congress of Vienna was being held, and increasingly during the next few years, nationalism was inspiring widespread agitation and revolts. In 1814 an attempt was made by Norwegians to set up an independent national state, with a king of their own choosing. It failed, but the Swedish king, on annexing the country, promised to respect Norway's constitution and internal autonomy.[2] In the same year a semisecret society, the Hetairia Philike, was founded for Greek national liberation.

Already the internal decay of the Ottoman Empire was being accelerated by the importation of Western nationalism through Napoleonic activities in Egypt and the Illyrian provinces, and British occupation of Greek ports and the Ionian islands, and also through Russian armed intervention. Serbian national rebellion against the Turks began in 1804, and, after successive suppression and renewal, it led to the establishment of Serbia's autonomy, under a native prince, in 1817. Then in 1821 began the Greek rebellion which especially appealed to both the classicism and the romanticism of western Europe, and to its liberal sentiments. Shelley and Keats addressed odes to the Greeks. Delacroix painted them in battle. Francis Lieber, young German patriot and long afterward a professor in Columbia College, enlisted and fought for them. Lord Byron died for them. In vain Metternich urged the European Great Powers to let the Greek revolt, like the Serbian, "burn itself out beyond the pale of European civilization." Great Britain and France joined Russia in compelling the Ottoman Empire to recognize in 1832 the independence of a small but national Greek state.

In the 1820's there were liberal nationalist outbreaks in Italy and

[1] For details see the excellent monograph by Hannah A. Straus, *Attitude of the Congress of Vienna Toward Nationalism in Germany, Italy and Poland* (1949).

[2] See John H. Wuorinen, "Scandinavia and the Rise of Modern National Consciousness," *Nationalism and Internationalism,* ed. by Edward M. Earle (1951).

Spain. They were repressed, but not so the revolt of the Spanish colonies on the American continents. In this instance nationalist Britain refused to cooperate with Metternich's "Concert of Europe" and backed the United States in proclaiming the famous "Monroe Doctrine."

In 1830–1831 a symbolic change occurred in France. The direct line of Bourbons that had been restored to the throne following Napoleon's downfall, while accepting certain principles of the French Revolution, had banned its flag and its anthem. Now, with forceful supplanting of the direct line of Bourbons with the Orleanist branch in the person of Louis Philippe, back came the revolutionary tricolor and "Marseillaise," and before long the new regime was encouraging a Napoleonic revival by pompous dedication of the Arc de Triomphe in honor of the emperor's victories and by solemn transport of his bones from faraway St. Helena to the crypt of the imposing Invalides on the bank of the Seine.

The revolutionary change in France was speedily followed by revolt of the Belgian Netherlands[1] against their Dutch king and of Poles against their Russian "king," the tsar. The former succeeded because it was supported by Great Britain and France. The latter failed because Russia, Austria, and Prussia made common cause against it. Lines appeared sharply drawn between western Europe where nationalism was political and militant, as well as cultural, and central and eastern Europe where the older institutions and practices of empire were exemplified by Austria, Russia, and Turkey.

3. Propaganda of Cultural Nationalism in Central and Eastern Europe

Yet, if hardly noticed at the time, cultural nationalism, intertwined with liberal and romantic movements, was making steady progress all over Europe during the first half of the nineteenth century. A

---

[1] The French-speaking (Walloon) population was foremost in the revolt against the Dutch. The Flemish (Dutch) half of Belgium, strongly Catholic, shared in the revolt more for religious than nationalist reasons. On the development of Flemish nationalism, there is an excellent monograph by Shepard B. Clough.

very influential prophet and preacher of it was Johann Gottfried von Herder (1744–1803), a half-pietist, half-rationalist Lutheran clergyman, disciple of Kant, admirer of Rousseau and of English romantic literature. He had been particularly impressed by the poetry of epic character which a Scot by the name of Macpherson published in English in the 1760's as a translation from the Gaelic of "Ossian," a reputed third-century bard. We now know that Ossian was mythical and that the poetry was the invention of Macpherson, but Herder and many of his contemporaries took it at face value, and from it Herder drew inspiration for his life-long interest in folk literature. During a five-year pastorate at Riga on the German-Russian border he started collecting and publishing folk verse in a variety of languages, and this he continued after settling at Weimar. Here, five years before the beginning of the French Revolution, he brought out his masterpiece, *Ideas on the Philosophy of the History of Mankind,* which constituted a veritable charter for nineteenth century cultural nationalism.

According to Herder, nationalities are most natural historic divisions of the human race. They are first differentiated from one another by peculiarities of geography and climate; then each develops distinctive language, literature, education, and customs, thereby becoming possessed of a "folk character," a kind of "national soul"; and so implanted in individuals is a particular national culture that they retain it for several generations after migrating to a foreign land. Herder urged the scientific study of anthropology and philology, as well as history, with the object of establishing a comparative "physiognomy" of the peoples of the world, and he implored intellectuals to apply such study to appreciation of the several national languages, literatures, religions, customs, costumes, and all other precious elements of cultural nationalism.

Herder evinced little interest in politics or political nationalism, and he died in 1803 before the national uprisings against Napoleon. Yet he inveighed against imperialism and the oppression of one people by another, and in the decades following 1815 his writings were regarded as sacred scripture by many an embryonic nationalist in

Metternich's Austrian Empire and elsewhere in central and eastern Europe.[1]

Along with Herder, other and younger German scholars and writers contributed to the vogue of cultural nationalism. For example, Friedrich von Schlegel (1772–1829) gave impetus to linguistic studies, maintaining that language indicates race and is the basis of nationality. Jacob Grimm (1785–1863) popularized national folk lore by indefatigable publication of German fairy tales and by resurrection of the old Teutonic mythology which, incidentally, was utilized by the nationalist Richard Wagner for his librettos. Friedrich von Savigny (1779–1861) pointed to folk law and folk custom as being, along with language, distinctive national possessions that should be treasured.

Simultaneously, much of historical writing, which in the eighteenth century had been classical in form and universal in appeal, became professedly "scientific" and purposefully nationalist.[2] Helpful to these ends was the monumental collection of source material for German history, projected by the patriotic Baron vom Stein and carried forward by a galaxy of patriotic German scholars including Pertz, Savigny, Humboldt, and Jacob Grimm. Similar editing of sources for English history began in a big way in the 1820's, and for French history, under the auspices of François Guizot, in the 1830's.

Music, too, became an important expression of romantic nationalist sentiment. One has only to contrast the eighteenth-century classical Gluck, Haydn, or Mozart with the later romantic Beethoven of the *Emperor Concerto* and *Ninth Symphony* to perceive what was happening. It is clearly manifest, from the 1820's through the 1840's in the German von Weber, the Franco-Polish Chopin, the Russian Glinka, in the Hungarian Rhapsodies of Liszt and the Tannhäuser and Lohengrin of Wagner.

[1] I have dealt with Herder at some length in an article in the *American Historical Review*, XXXII, 719–736 (1927); and a still fuller account is to be found in Robert R. Ergang's *Herder and the Foundations of German Nationalism* (1931).

[2] For English examples, see Thomas P. Peardon's *English Historiography, 1760–1830*.

Altogether, from 1814 onward, cultural nationalism not only was finding numerous exponents among German scholars and artists, not only was it being exemplified, as one might expect, in the national states of western Europe; it was permeating east-central and eastern Europe, especially among Slavic peoples. Here it was promoted by little groups of intellectuals—librarians, clergymen, closet professors—who in turn were patronized and subsidized by individual nobles and gentlemen as an avocation or a hobby. Paradoxically, these sponsors of nationalism in eastern Europe were usually of German nationality: they did not foresee the ultimate consequences. This they may be pardoned, since charitably disposed persons in general, including trustees of our present-day "Foundations," are usually innocent of what the "intellectuals" they subsidize may be up to.

To give here a detailed account of leading pioneers of cultural nationalism among the several peoples of central and eastern Europe would be pedantic and tiresome.[1] Let it suffice to offer some generalizations about them and their work. Among them was special concern for philology—for compilation of dictionaries and grammars, with the object of "purifying" an essentially peasant language and rendering it the vehicle for a national literature. There was similar concern for the collecting and publishing of folk ballads and legends, and for

[1] A detailed account would certainly deal with the careers of the following: Abbé Josef Dobrovský (1753–1829), Josef Jungmann (1773–1847), and František Palacký (1798–1876) among Czechs; Jan Kollár (1793–1852) and Pavel Šafařík (1795–1861) among Slovaks; Nikolai Karamzin (1766–1826) and Aleksander Pushkin (1799–1837) among Russians; Samuel Linde (1771–1847) and Adam Mickiewicz (1798–1855) among Poles; Vuk Karadžić (1787–1864) among Serbs; Bartholomäus Kopitar (1780–1844) among Slovenes; Ljudevit Gaj (1809–1871) among Croatians; Ferenc Kazinczy (1759–1831) and György Fejér (1766–1851) among Magyars; George Lazar (1779–1823) and Ioan Rădulescu (1802–1872) among Rumanians; Neophyt Rilski (1793–1881) among Bulgarians; Ivar Aasen (1813–1896), Henrik Wergeland (1808–1845), and Johan Welhaven (1807–1873) among Norwegians; and Elias Lönnrot (1802–1884) among Finns. Contemporaneous, in the 1830's and 1840's, was the Italian Risorgimento, marked in literature by Leopardi (1798–1837) and Manzoni (1785–1873), and by Count Cavour's newspaper. Some of the Slavs here mentioned are discussed in Hans Kohn's admirable *Panslavism* (1956). On the Norwegians and Finns, see respectively Oscar J. Falnes' *National Romanticism in Norway* and John H. Wuorinen's *Nationalism in Modern Finland*.

discovering or inventing national epics in the manner of the Gaelic Ossian, such as Kollár's *Slavic Daughter of Slava* or Lönnrot's Finnish *Kalevala* (1835); it was the latter's style and meter which Longfellow borrowed for his romantic American epic of *Hiawatha* (1855). There was concern, likewise, for folk history, for compiling source material, for celebrating legendary and national heroes and the pre-Christian and medieval past of one's people. Accompanying all these concerns, there was likely to be an atmosphere of romantic melancholy, with nostalgia for, and idealization of, "good old times" and far-off things. "The harp that once through Tara's Halls" was typical.

At first the cultural nationalism of the time was the work of individuals, patronized by individuals. Before long, however, groups of scholars and patrons formed Academies of Antiquities, of Language and Literature, of History. Then these Academies issued learned publications and semipopular magazines. Presently, a wide range of propagandist patriotic societies appeared, promoting folk costumes, patronizing folk dances and folk athletics, and fashioning folk banners and hymns.

4. Nationalism in Revolutions of 1848–1849

At the start, I have said, most scholarly advocates of *cultural* nationalism lacked *political* purpose. They might glorify a political state which this or that nationality had had in a more or less remote past, for example the medieval Holy Roman Empire "of the German Nation," or the fourteenth-century Yugoslav Empire of Stephen Dushan, but as a group they were notably unconcerned with contemporary politics. Soon, however, the movement for cultural nationalism was espoused by a growing number of politically-minded "liberals" (chiefly of the educated middle classes) who opposed the despotic regimes which Metternich supported and who sought by revolutionary means to establish, according to the English model, constitutional governments with guarantees of personal liberty. They argued that every nationality, as well as every individual, had an inherent right to freedom.

Such "liberal nationalists" were especially conspicuous during the
1830's and 1840's in Germany, Poland, and Italy. Mazzini, with his
Young Italy and Young Europe, was a fanatical and bombastic apostle
of the religion of liberal nationalism.[1] Existing states, he proclaimed,
must be overthrown and destroyed because God had prescribed
nationhood to every people, and in fulfilling this task the people—
the nationality—execute the divine will and incarnate themselves
with God in history; to Italy has fallen the holy mission of launching
the new order of mankind.

In 1848 a fierce thunderstorm of liberal nationalism broke over
Europe. Rioting was epidemic in Paris, Milan, Vienna, Berlin, Rome;
it was embryonic in Dublin and threatened in London. Metternich,
chased out of Vienna, took refuge in England.

Liberal constitutional governments were quickly set up in the Habs-
burg Empire for Germans, Czechs, and Hungarians, in the several
Italian states, in Prussia and most of the other German states, in
Denmark and the Netherlands. Simultaneously, a National Assembly
met at Frankfurt to arrange for the unification of Germany; a Pan-
Slavic Congress assembled at Prague; and plans were put forth for
Italian union or federation.[2]

Yet the storm passed with little apparent effect. The most significant thing about it was the conflict it raised between liberalism and
nationalism. For example, while all the revolutionary rulers in the
Habsburg Austrian Empire were professed liberals, they quarreled
and fought over national questions. Austrian German liberals, striving
to preserve traditional German domination of the polyglot Habsburg
Empire, forcefully and successfully resisted the efforts of Italian

[1] On Mazzini, see the contrasting but complementary volumes by Gaetano
Salvemini, new ed. (1956), and E. E. Y. Hales (1956). Hans Kohn in his
Prophets and Peoples, Studies in Nineteenth-Century Nationalism (1946) treats
of Mazzini, along with Mill and Michelet. Liberal nationalism is surveyed in
my *Historical Evolution of Modern Nationalism* (1931), ch. V, pp. 120–163.
One should not overlook the influence of Jeremy Bentham, which has been discussed in a monograph by Elmer L. Kayser (1932). Bentham, by the way,
coined the word "internationalism."

[2] Hans Kohn's *Pan-Slavism, Its History and Ideology* (1953) is a convenient
survey of the subject. Incidentally, his *Prophets and Peoples* (1940) contains a
discussion of Dostoyevsky's Russian nationalism.

liberals to unify their country. Magyar liberals, intent upon preserving intact the historic realm of Hungary, followed the leadership of the ultrapatriotic Louis Kossuth not only in demanding national independence for themselves but in denying the autonomous claims of their non-Magyar liberal subjects—Rumanian liberals in Transylvania and Slavic liberals in Croatia, Slovakia, and the Banat. Then the liberal Slavic Czechs and Slovenes of the Austrian crownlands, hitherto at odds with the German liberal regime at Vienna, joined it in fighting Kossuth's liberal Hungary, whose end was hastened by armed intervention of Slavic Russia.

The upshot by 1849 was the restoration of the unitary Habsburg Empire as it had been under Metternich, with apparent suppression of both liberalism and nationalism. The Pan-Slavic Congress at Prague, under the presidency of the Czech patriot and historian Palacký, proved a comic-tragic affair. The self-appointed delegates, finding that they couldn't understand one another in their different Slavic tongues, fell back on their common knowledge of German as the vehicle for drafting a rhetorical declaration of the assumed freedom-loving national character of Slavs. Whereupon the Congress came to a speedy and inglorious end with the shooting, by street rioters, of the wife and son of the German military governor of Bohemia, who, with perhaps pardonable ire, retaliated against the rioters and sent the Pan-Slavic delegates scurrying home.

Nor did success attend the effort of liberal Germans to create a unified national German state. In the Frankfurt Assembly they did adopt a nationalistic "Declaration of the Rights of the German Citizen" and a liberal constitution for a projected German Empire. But liberal Germany warred with liberal Denmark over the border provinces of Schleswig-Holstein, only to be stopped by the threat of Anglo-Russian intervention; and the resulting discomfiture of the Frankfurt Assembly was intensified by rivalry between Prussia and Austria, and finally completed by the restoration of conservative regimes in both those major states. Remnants of armed liberal opposition were crushed by Prussian troops in 1849, and the loose confederation of German states, under Austrian presidency, was reestablished.

5. The Third Napoleon as Nationalist, 1848–1870

I have just said that both liberalism and nationalism appeared to be crushed in the wake of the revolutionary storm of 1848. But the crushing was more apparent than real; temporary and episodic rather than decisive and permanent. Nationalism, though not immediately achieving the political goals which its leading advocates aspired to in Italy, Germany, or the Habsburg Empire, continued and actually gathered momentum as a kind of ground swell throughout central and east-central Europe. And it received new stimulation from France, the one country on the continent where the revolution of 1848 was followed, not by suppression, but by knight-errant championship, of nationalism.

The French revolution of 1848 had features reminiscent of the Jacobinism of the Great Revolution of 1789–1799. It dethroned Louis Philippe, the "bourgeois" king and last of French Bourbon monarchs, and it established a Second Republic with universal manhood suffrage. The democracy, thus proclaimed, was attended by a popular resurgence of nationalism. The expelled king and his prime minister had not been militantly patriotic. The new chief of state was the choice of an overwhelming majority of the democratic electorate, partly because he promised a regime of law and order, but chiefly because his name carried to the French masses a connotation of national glory. He was Prince Louis Napoleon Bonaparte, nephew of the general and emperor, and heir to the "Napoleonic Legend" which had been spun at St. Helena concerning the emperor's heroic efforts in behalf of peace and oppressed peoples.

Until recently it has been customary to accept Victor Hugo's estimate of Louis Napoleon as a charlatan and a "Little" Napoleon. But the prince was a good deal more than that. As President of the Second Republic for four years, and then for eighteen years more as Emperor of the French, under the title of Napoleon III, he dominated France longer than had any regime since that of the prerevolutionary monarchy. He was a consummate politician, one of the earliest practitioners of the arts and wiles of modern democratic government.

Until defeat in foreign war, he astutely managed to get support from a large majority of Frenchmen, whether conservatives or liberals, Catholics or agnostics, capitalists or workmen or peasants. His popular appeal was essentially nationalist—for the greater prosperity and the greater glory of France.

Napoleon III was a nationalist not only in regard to France. He was one on principle, dreaming of a Europe refashioned, under French tutelage, on the basis of self-determination for each nationality. Hence he was looked to for support by liberal patriots throughout the Continent, just as reactionary sovereigns had previously looked to Metternich. And like a knight-errant of nationalism, he repeatedly responded. To be sure, he combined with idealistic knight-errantry a politic ambition to obtain "compensations" of territory and prestige that would heighten French pride and strengthen his Empire.

The story of Napoleon III has been told many times and in great detail.[1] We here merely note his major efforts and achievements in the realm of nationalism. First, in alliance with Great Britain, he waged the Crimean War, thereby halting Russian aggression in the Near East, and then reasserting French primacy by having the peace congress held at Paris. From the Crimean War came, too, the Emperor's interest in the Rumanian people and his diplomatic moves that eventuated in the establishment of an independent Rumania.

Second, pressed by Cavour and other Italian patriots, he went to war with the Habsburg Empire and pushed its armies out of Lombardy. Thus was inaugurated the steady swift course by which, within two years, a free and united Italy came into being. As "compensation" for the services he rendered, Napoleon III obtained Savoy and Nice for France.

Third, the Emperor expressed sympathy for Polish national aspirations. He might have supported the Polish revolt of 1863 against Russia if the latter had not been backed by both Prussia and Austria and if his own forces had not been heavily engaged at the moment in Mexico.

Fourth, he reconstructed for France an overseas colonial empire.

[1] The best brief account is the late A. L. Guérard's (1957).

In the face of opposition from the United States, he failed, we know, to retain Mexico. But he succeeded in establishing French control of Algeria, Indo-China, and certain islands in the Pacific. This national imperialism of Napoleon III's foreshadowed what was to become, in the era after 1870, a conspicuous mark of nationalism among the great powers of Europe, and incidentally a prime means of exporting nationalism to other continents.

Finally, Napoleon III fatefully contributed to the creation of the nationalist Hohenzollern Empire of William I and Bismarck. His youthful schooling in a German gymnasium, his inherent romanticism, and his general interest in the principle of nationality, specifically exemplified in his concern with Italians, Rumanians, and Poles, all predisposed him to sympathize with the cause of German unification. He stood aside while Prussia fought it out with Austria in 1866 for German hegemony, imagining that victorious Prussia, under Bismarck, would "compensate" France by agreeing to its incorporation of Belgium or the Rhineland or at least Luxembourg. He was now aging, and the younger Bismarck outwitted and balked him at every turn. At last he acquiesced in popular French clamor for a showdown with Prussia (which was immediately provoked by Bismarck), and the ensuing Franco-Prussian War of 1870–1871 brought disaster to Napoleon III, and humiliation to France. The emperor lost his throne, and France lost Alsace-Lorraine, while in the Hall of Mirrors of Louis XIV's splendid palace at Versailles a glittering assemblage of German princes and generals hailed the Hohenzollern king of Prussia as emperor of a united—and very nationalist—Germany.

Napoleon III, though usually classed as a dictator, was a comparatively mild one. He had imbibed in his youth liberal and democratic ideas to which he at least paid lip service during his whole public career. He particularly adhered to the principle of national and democratic self-determination, holding popular plebiscites on fundamental matters of government within France and likewise on transfers of territory from one state to another. In unifying Italy, and in annexing Savoy and Nice to France, he saw to it that local inhabitants should be consulted and should approve by majority vote. He also got

Prussia to promise in 1866 that a similar plebiscite would be held in the duchy of Schleswig to determine whether it should be retained by Prussia or returned to Denmark, from which it had been seized.

The fall of Napoleon III and of France changed matters. Victorious Germany ignored the promised plebiscite in Schleswig, and annexed Alsace-Lorraine without consulting its inhabitants and against their clamorous protests. A new era was opening, marked throughout Europe by nationalism more blatant, more intolerant, and more forceful.

CHAPTER VII

Forceful Nationalism and
Industrialized Society
1864–1914

1. New and Competitive Militarism

The nationalism which swept like a tidal wave in the first two-thirds of the nineteenth century from western Europe over central and into eastern Europe, was associated and tinctured with the romantic liberalism of the era. Its political advocates held out to mankind an invigorating liberal promise—one which for a while seemed realizable—that every nationality should and would exercise a right of self-determination, ridding itself of alien control and imperialism, setting up a free national state of its own people. It would guarantee personal liberties to each citizen, establish parliamentary government, promote education, public works, and public health, and forward material well-being and prosperity. And as part of the prospect was the pleasant picture of peace between and among free national states and peoples. There would be free trade, free travel and migration, friendly rivalry in good works, limitation of armaments, judicial settlement of international disputes. A favorite subject for contemporary lithographs and amateur paintings was the lamb lying peacefully down with the lion. In 1842 Tennyson brought out *Locksley Hall,* containing its famous apostrophe to commerce and to the time when

"The war drum throbbed no longer and battle flags were furl'd
   In the Parliament of man, the Federation of the world."

In the next decade, however, Tennyson as Queen Victoria's Poet
Laureate was celebrating British bravery in charges of Heavy and
Light Brigades during the Crimean War, and writing of the British
defenders of Lucknow against the Indian sepoys:

"Handful of men as we were, we were English in heart
      and in limb
   Strong with the strength of the race to command, to
      obey, to endure."

And at the end of his long life, in *Locksley Hall Sixty Years After*, he
confessed to disillusionment about peace and progress and the Parliament of Man:

" 'Forward' rang the voices then, and of the many
      mine was one.
   Let us hush this cry of 'Forward' till ten thousand
      years have gone."

For meanwhile the events of 1848–1849 had indicated that to save
the lamb from the lion, to say nothing of federating the world, force
would be required. Not by simple and pacific self-determination
would the map of central and eastern Europe be redrawn along the
lines of nationality, but only through war, and then imperfectly.
The Crimean War of 1854–1856 inaugurated an independent and
united national state for Rumanians; the Franco-Austrian War of
1859, a like state for Italians. And the chief agent of both was Napoleon III, who, as we have seen, was a democrat and liberal of sorts,
and an exponent of the right of national self-determination.

Not so the foremost European statesman of the generation following Napoleon's. Otto von Bismarck was a nationalist of a different
kind; and the means he employed to erect and ensure a powerful
German Empire gave tone and character to the intensifying nationalism in Europe during the half century from 1864 to 1914. Bismarck

detested the Frankfurt Assembly of 1848 which had tried and failed to create a liberal, unified Germany. He stood for a national German state which would be dominated by his own conservative Prussia and from which Austria would be excluded. He would rely on the Prussian army, not on plebiscites, to achieve his ends.

Hence, against the opposition of German liberals, Bismarck fostered Prussian militarism. He arbitrarily established compulsory and effective army service for all able-bodied Prussians and triumphantly utilized it in three aggressive wars. First was the War of 1864, by which Denmark was ousted from the duchies of Schleswig-Holstein. Second was the Seven Weeks' War of 1866 by which the German Confederation that had been headed by Austria, and supported by most of the other German states, was destroyed and supplanted by a tighter federation dominated by an enlarged Prussia. Third was the Franco-Prussian War of 1870–1871, which not only ended the French Empire of Napoleon III but inaugurated the nationalistic German Empire of the Prussian Hohenzollerns by absorbing the South German states and appropriating from France the territory of Alsace-Lorraine.

"Nothing succeeds like success." Bismarck, from being in 1864 a most unpopular Prussian minister, became in the 1870's a hero of the German nation. There continued to be some dislike and criticism of his methods and policies on the part of minority groups in the German Empire, for example Socialists, Catholics, Radical Democrats, Poles, and Alsatians, but acclaim was loudly voiced by the majority parties of "National Liberals" and "Free Conservatives." His militarism, once resented, was now generally accepted both at home and abroad, for peacetime as well as for wartime. To uphold the prestige of the newly created German Empire among the European great powers, and to safeguard it against any "war of revenge" by France, Bismarck insisted that it must retain, and from time to time increase, the size and efficiency of its armed forces—and it did so.

The Austrian Empire, after its defeat by Prussia in 1866, and its resulting extrusion from both Germany and Italy, sought to conciliate the vociferously nationalist Magyars by transforming itself from a centralized state into a "dual monarchy," of which the Habsburg ruler would be emperor of German Austria (with its subject Czechs and Slovenes) and king of Magyar Hungary (with its subject Croats and Slovaks and Rumanians). The partnership represented a German-Magyar alliance against disruptive tendencies of Slavic nationalism, and one of the first acts of the Dual Monarchy of Austria-Hungary was the adoption of the Prussian system of compulsory conscription for its joint armies.

France, as an outcome of its defeat by Prussian German arms, supplanted Napoleon III with the Third French Republic. But Republican France was as nationalist as Imperial France; losing Alsace-Lorraine to Germany, it took from Germany the Prussian army system. At least on paper, Russia, and Italy too, followed the German example in the early 1870's and introduced universal conscription.

Only Great Britain, among major countries of Europe, stuck to the professional long-service army. Yet even the pacific Gladstone, who was prime minister at the time, was not proof against the militarism which flooded the Continent in the wake of the Franco-Prussian War. Lord Cardwell, his able war secretary, vigorously and radically reformed the professional army, while Britain's naval superiority was amply maintained. And the attendant heightening of British nationalism expressed itself in the general election of 1874, which deposed Gladstone in favor of the imperialistic and rather jingoistic Disraeli. If the king of Prussia was now an emperor, why, thought Disraeli, shouldn't England's Queen be an empress? So, in flattery to her and for Britain's glory, Victoria was proclaimed Empress of India.

Though the European great powers managed to preserve an "armed peace" between each other during the years from 1871 to 1914, the period was repeatedly punctuated by nationalist wars which affected the balance of power and exacerbated national rivalry. In 1875 both Bulgarians and Bosnian Serbs rose in arms against the Ottoman Empire. Followed the Russo-Turkish War of 1877–1878, concluding with expansion of Russia in Bessarabia and the Caucasus, recognition of full independence of Serbia and Rumania and autonomy for Bulgaria, and, in the nature of consolation prizes for Austria-Hungary and Great

Britain, the "military occupation" of Bosnia-Herzegovina by the former and of Cyprus by the latter.

In 1885 Serbia warred with Bulgaria. In 1897 Greece fought to obtain Crete from the Turks. In 1898 was waged the Spanish-American War, and from 1899 to 1902 the war between British and Dutch in South Africa. Failure marked the International Peace Conferences at The Hague in 1899 and 1907. Instead there came in quickening succession the Russo-Japanese War of 1904–1905, the Italian-Turkish War of 1911–1912, the two Balkan Wars of 1912–1913—and the terrible World War I of 1914–1918.

Militarism did not keep the peace, as its proponents sometimes argued it would. But it did stimulate and gravely heighten nationalist fervor in Europe and throughout traditional Christendom.

2. Effects of Industrial Revolution

Modern nationalism had arisen in a preponderantly agricultural and commercial society. Its original champions had belonged to the landed gentry or to the professional middle class of traders, lawyers, civil servants, scholars, and journalists. As for the masses, those in rural areas seem to have been less responsive than those in urban centers where intercommunication was relatively easy and means of propaganda more available. Such had notably been the case in the England of the sixteenth and seventeenth centuries, and also in revolutionary France of the late eighteenth century. Much the same social pattern underlay the spread of cultural and then political nationalism in central and eastern Europe during the first two-thirds of the nineteenth century.

In the last third of the century, however, the development of technology and large-scale machine industry—what we call the "Industrial Revolution"—was transforming the traditional pattern of European society and laying foundation for a more rampant nationalism. To be sure, the revolution had gotten under way in England in the eighteenth century, and by 1848 it was already beginning to furnish the European Continent—and the United States—with steam-powered factories and locomotives, with railway lines and telegraph wires. But outside of England the social and national consequences of the revolution were not widely or deeply impressive until the 1860's and 1870's. Then the shift of population from farm to factory, from countryside to city, from peasantry to "proletariat," grew apace. So did the means of transportation and communication; so, too, the rivalry of peoples for economic advantage.

All this had bearing on the nationalist struggles of the time. It was England's industrial primacy which was mainly responsible for her triumph over Revolutionary and Napoleonic France, and also for the mighty prestige she enjoyed for at least a century afterward. Moreover, the American Civil War of 1861–1865, the longest and most destructive struggle in the hundred years from Napoleon to the First World War, was won by the more industrialized and hence wealthier North; and it resulted not only in "preserving" the Union but in establishing its coercive supremacy over the several states. It was likewise the more industrialized Germany which defeated France in 1870–1871 and wrested from her the provinces of Alsace-Lorraine. And without increasing and spreading industrialization, it would have been impossible to maintain the mounting competitive armaments which major nations possessed from the 1860's and 1870's. An industrial nation could now be, indeed, a "great power." On the other hand, industrial backwardness might be calamitous, as indicated by successive defeats and losses of the Ottoman Empire in 1877–1878 and 1911–1913, of Spain in 1898, and of the South African Boers in 1899–1902.

One might suppose, as many a Liberal has done, that the spread of the Industrial Revolution would favor and increase commercial intercourse between nations, thereby bringing about a widening acceptance of free trade and a broadening cooperation among peoples. It undoubtedly magnified international trade and contacts. Yet it proved to be even more conducive to internal national trade and development. Exports and imports of an industrialized nation did not normally equal in value what it bought and sold at home. Credit and banking functioned nationally far more than internationally.

Labor, including unionized labor and even Socialist labor, was organized by nations, and if it had international affiliations it subordinated them to what it considered to be its particular national interests. There was much more travel by people within a nation than between nations. There was more news in the public press about one's own nation than about others. Schooling was organized and conducted on a national, not an international, basis.

Possibly if the whole world could have been industrialized simultaneously and uniformly, with the same standard of living prevailing everywhere, national differences might not have been emphasized, and full economic liberalism, with its promise of "peace and universal brotherhood," might have been realized. What a Utopian dream! Actually, no two countries have been at any given time in exactly the same stage of industrialization, and especially after 1880 each partially industrialized country utilized the sentiment of nationalism and the power of national government to protect by tariffs and bounties its own industry against foreign competition, and by labor legislation and restriction of foreign immigration to raise the standard of living of its own people.

This is the *economic nationalism* which was significantly pursued by Bismarckian Germany and by post-Civil-War United States.[1] It has since been adopted and applied by nation after nation. It is basic to the "welfare state," as exemplified by Germany in the 1880's, by Great Britain in the early 1900's, by the United States in the 1930's, and, in most drastic form, by Communist Russia.

In fine, the Industrial Revolution served in many ways to spread and intensify nationalism. It increased the wealth and power of national states in Europe and America where it began and chiefly developed. It accentuated economic rivalry among them, and it contributed to a competitive imperialism which led eventually to nationalist reaction in Asia and Africa. For among "backward" countries outside Europe, as among subject peoples within, the introduction of machinery, railways, and other features of the Industrial Revolu-

[1] I have discussed this economic nationalism in Chapter VII of the *Historical Evolution of Modern Nationalism* (1931).

tion aroused and stimulated an ambition to emulate the industrialized and imperialistic nations of the West and to seek prosperity and strength in national independence and economic nationalism. First and foremost to achieve such an ambition was Japan. Here, from the 1870's onward, both material industrialization and nationalist spirit were imported from Europe and so successfully fused and implanted as to render Japan, in a surprisingly short time, a "great power." It had the might and the national will to overwhelm China in 1894–1895 and to trounce Russia in 1904–1905.

Industrialized national states, with their greatly augmented financial resources, have been enabled with increasing rapidity since 1880 to carry to unforeseen lengths certain developments which the Jacobin nationalists of the French Revolution had dreamed of and experimented with: egalitarian democracy; public schooling, as well as military training, of the masses; cheap popular journalism; efficient societies for popular propaganda. To these we next attend.

3. Mass Migration, Democracy, and Literacy[1]

A striking effect of the Industrial Revolution was its dislocation of the masses. In earlier agricultural society the masses had been relatively settled in body and mind. Now, industrial demands and opportunities rendered them migratory, nomadic, almost gypsy-like. They moved from country to country, from farm to city, from city to city, from one tenement to another. A vast and growing number of them thus became what the French call *déracinés*, uprooted from ancestral soil, from long established habit and tradition. Furthermore, the first and second generations of such migrants usually experienced an extraordinary economic insecurity, which was apt to produce psychological maladjustment. Huddled as most of them now were in overgrown towns, they were not only peculiarly exposed to demagoguery of one sort or another, but they had special incentive and means for agitating for betterment of their lot.

[1] Parts of this and of the next section are taken, in condensed form and with publisher's permission, from my *Generation of Materialism, 1871–1900* (copyright by Harper & Brothers, 1941).

The prime means was trade unionism, which, originating among industrial workers in Great Britain, accompanied the development of machine industry and resulting growth of cities in Europe and America. Chiefly through strikes or threats of strike and through mass pressure on governments, it strove for higher wages, shorter working hours, restriction of competitive labor of women and children, and better working conditions. Gradually it secured for itself full legalization, in Britain, for instance, in 1871, and in France in 1884. Above all, it proved to be a major factor in shifting the trend of public interest and opinion from the economic liberalism of the mid-nineteenth century to the economic nationalism of the last quarter of the century. It was truly an urban mass movement and a potent advocate of mass democracy and mass education.

Hardly less influential was the cooperative movement which industrialization fostered. Cooperative stores and shops, "friendly societies" and fraternal orders, cooperative loan banks and credit societies and cooperative dairies spread and multiplied. Thereby farmers and lower middle classes, as well as industrial workers, were advantaged and brought into closer and more interdependent contact.

Political democracy, with extension of voting rights to the masses, marked the era after 1870. Its coming was due to several causes: agitation of trade unionists and cooperatives; rival bidding of political parties or factions for broader popular support; appeal of the concept and slogan of "progress"; logical application of liberal and Christian principles of individualism and humanitarianism. In Britain, Conservatives and Liberals vied with each other in establishing well-nigh universal manhood suffrage between 1867 and 1885. In the United States, as an outcome of the Civil War, slavery was abolished and in 1870 Negroes were at least theoretically enfranchised. France, which had had a form of manhood suffrage since 1848, confirmed and applied it under the Third Republic from 1871. Even the Conservative Bismarck consented to democratic election of the lower legislative house (*Reichstag*) of his newly created German Empire. In other European countries, adoption of universal manhood suffrage kept pace with advancing industrialization: in Belgium in 1894, in Norway in 1898, in Italy, Austria, Sweden, and Spain in 1907. Democracy was a goal of revolutionary movements, between 1904 and 1912, in the Russian and Ottoman Empires, in Persia, Portugal, Mexico, and the Chinese Empire. It seemed to be a world-wide "wave of the future." At any rate, the United States went to war in 1917, in the memorable words of Woodrow Wilson, "to make the world safe for democracy."

Closely following the extension of the franchise to the masses was the spread of literacy among them. As we have seen, the French Revolution had laid plans for elementary state schooling for everybody, and Napoleon had started to give effect to them.[1] But they were then halted by exigencies of war and shortage of funds. It required heavy public expenditure to build and maintain free schools for the masses, and not until a nation's wealth was materially multiplied by the Industrial Revolution could it afford the necessary cost.

This occurred in one country after another, mainly after 1870. As late as the 1860's a third of Great Britain's adult population and three-fifths of France's could not read or write, while in the United States almost all Negroes and a considerable number of whites were illiterate. But by 1914, every country, in measure as it had undergone industrialization, possessed a system of elementary and secondary schools and a generally literate population.

What induced the governing classes of the period to favor mass education, and to provide needful taxation for it, was not simply a humanitarian impulse. It was a variety of motives: response of the politician to demands of the masses; logical application of the liberal doctrine of individual rights; belief of the democrat that wise participation of the masses in government required their schooling; notion of the reformer and moralist, as expressed by Guizot, that "the opening of a schoolhouse closes a jail." The transcendent urge, however, was nationalist. It was to unify a people, by belittling their economic, social, occupational, and religious differences, and by emphasizing their national language and the inculcation of a common national patriotism.

[1] See above, pp. 53, 59.

However one may judge the results of public mass schooling, there can be no doubt that its nationalist purpose has been well served.[1] It has been replete with patriotic teaching and observance, and there seems to be in most countries a direct proportion between the degree of popular literacy and that of unquestioning national loyalty. At the time of World War I, when most of the common soldiers in Russian armies were illiterate, they eventually got tired of fighting, disobeyed their officers, threw down their arms, and set off for home. During World War II, when the Russian mass armies were largely literate, they obeyed the national authorities and fought valiantly through one reverse after another until ultimate victory. Of course in the latter case it may have been Messianic devotion to Communism, as much as national spirit, which animated the Russian masses. In any case, the Russian soldiers of the 1940's, unlike their fathers, could read and write—and they had been more uniformly indoctrinated.

With mass schooling came journalism for the masses. Prior to 1880 European newspapers had usually been slight affairs of a few pages, representing personal or party opinion, limited in circulation to a local clientele among the middle and upper classes, and relatively high priced. A very few, such as the London *Times*, the Paris *Temps* or *Journal des Débats*, the Vienna *Neue Freie Presse*, or the New York *Tribune*, had national and even international repute, but none of them enjoyed what we would now describe as mass circulation.

The rise of really cheap, popular journalism after 1880 resulted from (1) improved means of news-gathering and printing, (2) increased income from industrial advertising, (3) enactment of liberal press laws, and (4) most important, editorial catering to the newly literate masses. Within a score of years (1880–1900), the number of European journals doubled, mainly in countries of growing industry and literacy. By 1900 *Le Petit Journal* of Paris had a mass circulation of two million, the *Lokal Anzeiger* of Berlin a million, and the *Daily*

[1] See Jonathan Scott's *Patriots in the Making* (1916); W. C. Langsam's "Nationalism and History in the Prussian Elementary Schools Under William II," *Nationalism and Internationalism*, ed. by E. M. Earle (1951); C. J. H. Hayes, *France, a Nation of Patriots* (1930), pp. 35–63, 343–408; Bessie Pierce, *Citizens' Organizations and the Civic Training of Youth* (1933).

Mail and the *Daily Express* of London had circulations of over a million each. In the United States, Hearst's *American* was vying with Pulitzer's *World* for mass readers; between them they had already been a prime factor in inciting the American public to war with Spain.[1]

To reach the largest possible number of readers, the newer type of journal avoided long words which the masses might not understand, and controversial subjects which might offend any large segment of the masses. It stressed the sensational rather than the factual: sports and "funnies" and "feature articles," rather than straight prosaic news; local and national affairs, rather than foreign or international. It was apt to be stridently patriotic, even jingoistic. As such it supplemented and reinforced the work of national state schools.

What a profusion of patriotic societies attended popular journalism and schooling, and what propaganda they contributed! In an industrialized country, one had only to get a financial backer (an "angel") and equip an office with typewriter, telephone, stenographer, mimeograph, and filing cabinet, in order to become organizer and director of some sort of society that in due course would have a big membership and be self-supporting. There were societies for war veterans, for sons and daughters of veterans, for every conceivable patriotic and national purpose.[2]

Nationalism, to be sure, was not the only "ism" which secured popular following and conducted popular propaganda in the era of industrialization, mass migration, and mass literacy. There was pacifism, for instance, and internationalism, and various types of humanitarianism. Especially in industrial cities on the European Continent, Marxian socialism had a notable vogue among displaced and restless workingmen, as well as among groups of middle-class "intellectuals." This was a kind of religion itself, and doctrinally it professed to be cosmopolitan and antinational. Yet by 1900, under the influence of a "reformist" right-wing, it was becoming in western Europe a

[1] See Walter Millis, *The Martial Spirit* (1931).
[2] An interesting British example is amusingly treated by Janet H. Robb in her *Primrose League* (1941).

democratic rather than revolutionary force and evincing patriotic attachments.[1]

4. Materialism and Nationalism

We must not lose sight of certain philosophical effects of the technology and science of the era from 1870 to 1914. At the beginning of the era, there had been no practical use of electricity, except for the telegraph; no dynamos or telephones or wireless. There were no Kodaks or movies; no gasoline engines, and hence no automobiles or airplanes or military tanks; no significant oil or rubber industries; and comparatively little steel production. All these, which are so basically and vitally important to us nowadays, were developed during the generation that followed 1870 and preceded World War I.

Moreover, all these developed as machines, or else machines developed them. In an astonishingly brief time, Europe and America—and Japan—became a machine-world. No wonder that ordinary men's minds were obsessed with mechanical and technological progress. This seemed more immediately important and much more promising to the practical well-being of a nation than any historic or supernatural religion.

The materialism and religious skepticism of the age were increased, especially among intellectuals, by the vogue of certain scientific doctrines. One was the elaboration of the Newtonian physics of the seventeenth century, with general acceptance of "matter" as something solid and substantial, something composing the universe and operating according to simple mechanical laws. Of course physical science as thus conceived was subsequently revolutionized, and rendered far more complex—and dubious—through the work of Einstein, Planck, and others, but the philosophic bearing of the "new physics" has been only slowly and imperfectly grasped. A strictly mechanical and materialist conception of the universe and of human life had been too deeply and widely implanted.

[1] See, for example, *Jean Jaurès, a Study of Patriotism in the French Socialist Movement* by the late Harold Weinstein (1936), or an article of mine, "German Socialism Reconsidered," *American Historical Review*, XXIII, 62–101 (1917).

A second influential doctrine of the era was that of the biological evolution associated with the name of Charles Darwin. There was, to be sure, no novelty about the general idea of evolution: it had been entertained by ancient Greeks, by a Christian theologian such as St. Augustine, and by a scientist of the "enlightenment" such as J. B. Lamarck. Besides, the Darwinian doctrine of evolution through a process of "natural selection," with "inheritance of acquired characteristics," has since been considerably modified in the light of the heredity principles experimentally tested by the monk, Gregor Mendel, and of the doubts cast by August Weismann on the inheritance of acquired traits. Nevertheless, from Darwin's time onward, evolution (with or without amendment) was ever more widely accepted as explanatory of the origin of man—and, indeed, of all creation. Ernst Haeckel, a devoted and imaginative Darwinian, outlined to a scientific congress at Cambridge University in 1898 man's evolution in twenty-six stages from chunks of carbon through simple structureless bits of protoplasm and on through chimpanzee and *pithecanthropus erectus*. And a swarm of philosophers and sociologists, headed by Herbert Spencer, used Darwinism to explain social as well as biological phenomena; from it they derived and applied those fearful slogans, "the struggle for existence" and "survival of the fittest." At the same time, one was optimistically led to believe that everything was being evolved by natural and material process from a lower to a higher plane.

There was also the doctrine of physiological psychology, as enunciated by Wilhelm Wundt and preached by numerous disciples. It assumed that man is like any other animal, that he has no peculiar or distinctive "soul" but only an "animal mind," and that his behavior can be predicated on laboratory study of animal "reflexes" and "reactions." Here was a belittling of reason, a belittling which was further emphasized by the later Freudian psychology, with its stress on the unconscious and on sex motivation.

Marxism was not merely a movement of protest against social injustice. It was a reflection and embodiment of the materialism of the age, and leading disciples of Karl Marx were fond of likening the "evolutionary materialism" of his "scientific" socialism (or communism) to that of Darwin.

The materialist and mechanistic trend of the time provided favorable environment for a cult of bigness, not only bigness of business, but bigness of nations. That nation was deemed greatest, not by reason of its possessing the highest culture, but because it had the most material things—greatest wealth, greatest buildings, greatest manufactures, greatest commerce, greatest army and navy, greatest colonial empire. These things could be boasted about. They made a nation a really great power and enabled it to play power politics. They gave impetus to bellicose, expansionist nationalism.

Nationalist propagandists of a superheated sort naturally seized upon the pseudoscientific generalization about the "struggle for existence and survival of the fittest" for the exalting of the force and praise of "heroic virtue." As the German General Friedrich von Bernhardi wrote in a "best-seller" of 1912: "The struggle for existence is, in the life of Nature, the basis of all healthy development. All existing things show themselves to be the result of contesting forces. So in the life of man the struggle is not merely the destructive, but the life-giving principle. . . . War gives a biologically just decision, since its decisions rest on the very nature of things. . . . To expand the idea of the National State into that of humanity, and thus to entrust apparently higher duties to the individual, leads to error, since in a human race conceived as a whole, struggle and, by implication, the most essential vital principle would be ruled out. Any action in favor of collective humanity outside the limits of the State and Nationalism is impossible. Such conceptions belong to the wide domain of Utopias."

Also, in a book published in the same year, the ex-chancellor of the German Empire, Bernhard von Bülow, wrote: "In the struggle between nations, one nation is the hammer and the other the anvil; one is the victor and the other the vanquished. . . . If ever the battle between the higher and lower civilization should cease in the world's history, our belief in the further development of mankind would lose its foundation. . . . We must remember Moltke's words: 'Permanent peace is a dream, and not even a beautiful one,' but 'war is an essential element of God's scheme of the world.'"[1]

Even more dithyrambic was a professor of psychology at Harvard, the German-American Hugo Münsterberg. In a volume he brought out in 1914, he proclaimed his belief in "the fundamental law of five thousand years of history that ultimately the life needs of healthy nations are decisive, . . . that only war can adjust the power of countries to the changing stages of their inner development. . . . It is easily said, and the average American likes to say it, that nations ought to respect the possessions of other nations as individuals respect the private property of their neighbors. But this apparently highest morality would be the grossest immorality. . . . A victorious war may bring to a nation a complete regeneration—the moral energies awake; vice is repressed; life is protected; education flourishes; hygiene spreads; science rebuilds the land; prosperity grows; temperance and self-discipline prevail; family life can expand in the new abundance"!

Such paeans were not chanted solely by German patriots. For instance there was the patriotic Englishman J. A. Cramb, professor at the University of London, who outdid even Münsterberg. "The friendship of nations," he wrote in 1914, "is an empty name; peace is at best a truce on the battlefield of Time; the old myth or the old history of the struggle for existence is behind us, but the struggle for power—who is to assign bounds to its empire, or invent an instrument for measuring its intensity? . . . In Europe, which really governs the planet, every advance in politics or religion has been attended by war. . . . for the peace which Christ came to proclaim was not the peace of the ending of battles; it was the peace within the soul, the spirit at one with itself, Islam in the sense that Mohammed used it, a metaphysical peace altogether apart from political peace." In conclusion the English professor rises to mystical heights. "In war and the right of war," he says, "man has a possession which he values

[1] The Moltke here quoted by Bülow in 1912 was Chief of the Prussian General Staff from 1858 until 1888 and commander during the victorious wars with Denmark (1864), Austria (1866), and France (1870–1871). He died in 1891.

above religion, above industry and above social comforts; in war man values the power which it affords to life of rising above life, the power which the spirit of man possesses to pursue the Ideal . . . and which transcends reason."

Transcends reason! Here is nationalism as a spiritual force, a veritable religion, belligerent and expansive and intolerant.

It is this kind of nationalism—a kind which I have elsewhere described as "integral"[1]—which flourished throughout traditional Christendom in the decades after 1870. It was a response to the industrialism and materialism of the age, and to the pseudoscientific propaganda which was spread nationally through the new mass movements, the new mass education, and the new mass journalism. It attended—and inspired—the nationalist imperialism and intolerance of which we treat in the following chapter. It eventuated, as a succeeding chapter shows, in world wars of the present century.

[1] *Historical Evolution of Modern Nationalism* (1931), ch. VI.

CHAPTER VIII

Nationalist Imperialism and Intolerance
1874–1914

1. Outburst of National Imperialism

At the very time, from the 1870's to World War I, when nationalism was being intensified by industrialization and was becoming a truly mass movement in Europe and America,[1] there was an extraordinary outburst of national imperialism. Europe's earlier commercial and colonial imperialism had seemed in the 1860's to be declining, and its speedy disappearance was then predicted by such doughty English Liberals as Cobden and Bright. France, a century previously, had lost an extensive colonial empire in America and India; recently, Napoleon III's project of dominating Mexico had been thwarted. Britain, too, had been forced in the eighteenth century to part with its most populous and most promising colonies in America; and since then it had conceded self-government to Canada, Australia, New Zealand, and South Africa. The Portuguese and the bulk of the Spanish Empires in the New World had been transformed into independent nations.

Imperialistic revival and expansion began in a big way in 1874 with the advent of Disraeli's Conservative ministry in Great Britain. A group of Pacific islands, bearing the exotic name of Fiji, was im-

[1] Parts of this chapter are taken, in condensed form and with permission of the publisher, from my *Generation of Materialism, 1871–1900* (copyright by Harper & Brothers, 1941).

mediately added to the British Empire, and a British protectorate was established over native states in the Malay peninsula. The next year Disraeli sensationally purchased control of the Suez Canal for Britain, a first step in British subjugation of Egypt. Within the next five years he incorporated into British India the large khanate of Baluchistan, took from the Ottoman Empire the Mediterranean island of Cyprus, and warred against Afghans in Asia and Zulus in South Africa. In this latter conflict, by a curious twist of fate, the son and heir of Napoleon III was slain.

France followed the British example in the early 1880's, under the leadership of Jules Ferry. The Pacific island of Tahiti was annexed. Protectorates were established over Tunisia and Madagascar. French Indo-China was enlarged and consolidated. Foundations were laid for the construction of French West Africa and French Equatorial Africa.[1]

Bismarck at first opposed overseas imperialism for Germany. In the mid-1880's, however, responding to public pressure from German explorers, businessmen, and patriots, he finally inaugurated a far-flung German domain that comprised Togoland and the Cameroons in western Africa, large tracts of Southwest Africa and East Africa, part of the Malayan island of New Guinea (piously christened "Kaiser Wilhelms Land") and a group of other Pacific islands (renamed, with like piety, the "Bismarck Archipelago").

Also in the 1880's, King Leopold II of Belgium appropriated the vast "Congo Free State"; and two Italian statesmen, Depretis and Crispi, in turn secured for their country East African territories of Eritrea and Somaliland. Incidentally, Crispi's ensuing attempt to conquer for Italy the ancient Kingdom of Ethiopia was successfully resisted on the battlefield of Adowa. It was an almost unique setback to European imperialism.

Simultaneously, the ultraconservative and nationalist Tsar Alexander III pressed the expansion of the Russian Empire in the Caucasus, in Turkestan, and on the frontiers of China. Then in the

[1] For details, see Thomas F. Powers' *Jules Ferry and French Imperialism* (1942).

1890's both Japan and the United States embarked on overseas imperialism. Japan wrested Korea and Formosa from China. The United States, under the presidency of William McKinley and with the strenuous backing of Theodore Roosevelt (and popular, patriotic journalism), annexed Hawaii and part of Samoa and forcefully acquired Puerto Rico and the Philippines.

Nor did the wave of European (and American and Japanese) national imperialism reach its crest at the dates just indicated. These only marked its rise. It rolled on, gathering ever greater momentum and power, until World War I. By this time, almost all of the African Continent and of islands throughout the globe's oceans, together with most of the vast expanse and teeming millions of Asia, were parceled out among European powers as outright possessions, protectorates, or "spheres of influence." It then seemed as though the whole world was destined to be "Europeanized."

It has often been argued, especially by Marxists, that the newer imperialism of 1874–1914 was an economic phenomenon, a natural and inevitable product of the Industrial Revolution and the capitalism it fostered. Certainly the Revolution's improved means of transportation and communication, and of warfare, rendered easier the acquisition and holding of "backward" areas, and doubtless large-scale mechanized industry stimulated an ever-widening quest for markets where surplus manufactures might be disposed of, raw materials procured, and lucrative investments made.

Yet the economic explanation is not fully convincing. Neither Russia nor Italy had surplus manufactures to dispose of or surplus wealth to invest, though both engaged in the scramble for imperial dominion. Germany acquired an extensive colonial empire before she had much exportable capital, and France obtained an even bigger overseas empire while her industrial development lagged behind Germany's. Great Britain had long had all the supposed economic motives for imperialism—export of manufactured goods, demand for raw materials, supply of surplus capital—though these did not move her in the 1850's and 1860's as they did in the '70's and '80's. On the other hand, Norway, whose ocean-borne commerce was exceeded only by Britain's and Germany's, remained consistently aloof from overseas imperialism.

Besides, however much the participating nations may have expected to reap from the new imperialism in financial gain, their expenditure on army, navy, and administration for it chronically exceeded their direct income from it. And we may doubt whether much of the wealth which accrued to individual traders and investors, even to a Cecil Rhodes or a King Leopold, could not have been obtained without the political dominion which proved very costly and in the long run provocative of world unrest and native revolts.

2. *Nationalism, Seed and Product of the New Imperialism*

Basically, the new imperialism was a nationalistic phenomenon. It followed hard upon the national wars which created a powerful Germany and a united Italy, which carried Russian arms within sight of Constantinople, and which deprived France of Alsace-Lorraine and alarmed Britain. It expressed a resulting psychological reaction, an ardent desire on the part of statesmen to maintain or recover national prestige. France sought compensation for European loss in oversea gain. Britain would offset her European isolation by enlarging the British Empire. Russia, halted in the Balkans, would expand anew in Asia. Germany and Italy would show that the prestige they had won by national unification inside Europe they were entitled to enhance by imperial exploits outside. The United States would veil dread memories of its Civil War by uniting North and South in war against Spain and faraway Filipinos. The lesser European powers, with no great prestige at stake, managed, with the possible exception of Belgium, to get on without any new imperialism, though Portugal and the Netherlands displayed a revived pride in the empires they already had, and the latter's was administered with renewed vigor.

To enlist popular and governmental support for imperialism, numerous patriotic societies sprang up and conducted propaganda of their own or abetted that of nationalist newspapers. Such propaganda stressed a number of "reasons." A prominent one was "protection": protection of the flag and "honor" of one's nation; protection of one's fellow nationals, whether traders or missionaries or mere adventurers. For example, the murder of two Christian missionaries of German nationality by a band of Chinese thugs in Shantung province in 1897 led immediately to landing of German marines and to the dispatch from Germany of a supporting naval and military expedition amid frenzied huzzas and grandiloquent exchange of toasts between its commander, Prince Henry, and his brother, Emperor William II. Said the Emperor: "May it be clear out there to the German merchant, and above all to the foreigner whose soil we may be on and with whom we shall have to deal, that the German Michael has planted his shield, adorned with the eagle of the Empire, firmly on that soil, in order once for all to afford protection to those who apply to him for it. . . . Should anyone attempt to affront us or to infringe our good rights, then strike out with mailed fist." The two dead missionaries were duly avenged. China was compelled to lease the port of Kiaochow to Germany and to recognize the entire province of Shantung as a German "sphere of influence." And, of course, the sound of German guns was the signal for appropriation of still other Chinese ports and regions by Russia, France, and Great Britain in "protection" of their respective national interests.

National imperialism was likewise defended as a humanitarian movement in behalf of higher civilization. It was the white man's "burden," or his "manifest destiny," to clean up areas infested with yellow fever and cholera and other human scourges and to bring to backward peoples the blessings of order and sanitation and schooling and science and material "progress"; in a word, to "uplift" mankind. The British particularly claimed that a prime objective of their imperial sway was the training of native peoples for some degree of self-government, eventually perhaps for national independence.

There was also the contention, in view of an extraordinary increase of Europe's population in the wake of the Industrial Revolution, that an overseas colonial empire might attract a goodly part of the increase. Thereby European emigrants would be deflected from a country, say the United States, where they would lose their national language and loyalty, to colonies where they would retain them. Despite arguments and urgings of the kind, comparatively few emigrants actually settled in Africa and almost none in Asia; the bulk of them continued to seek homes in America amid less exotic surroundings and greater economic opportunities. However, such as did settle in this or that colonial empire were apt to be more nationalist and imperialist than their fellow nationals in Europe. Thus, French settlers in Algeria showed themselves more eager than the government at Paris to secure the annexation of adjacent African lands to France. British settlers in South Africa had almost a psychosis about any possible foreign encroachment, and from them, rather than from London, came the main drive for British expansion northward. Australian and New Zealand colonials constantly pressed the home government to forestall alien seizure of South Sea islands.

Presumably a colonial empire increased the mother country's war potential, not only through its own settlers and administrators, but also through a trained native soldiery such as the British developed in India and the French in Indo-China and West Africa. Overseas imperialism certainly gave a special boost to naval building and naval competition. Warships were needed for colonial defense, and the more warships there were, and the farther they had to go, the greater was the need for "coaling stations" en route—which, in turn, meant additional colonies.

In certain instances, flags of European imperial powers were seemingly hoisted by an explorer or ship captain as a national competitive sport with about the same indifference to any practical consideration as characterized the later planting of American and other flags on cakes of ice around the North or South Pole. As one reads of successive French flag raisings in oases of the Sahara and on sunbaked atolls of the Pacific, one gets a lively impression that it was all *pour le sport national.*

The new national imperialism involved much policing of the world by the powers concerned, and many wars. There were wars of subjugation, for instance, against Algerians in the 1870's, against Bur-

mese in the '80's, against Sudanese in the '80's, and '90's, against
Ethiopians in the '90's, Chinese "Boxers" at the turn of the century,
and Filipinos in the 1900's. Likewise there were international wars:
the Franco-Chinese, the Sino-Japanese, the Spanish-American, the
Anglo-Boer, the Russo-Japanese, the Italo-Turkish. And there was
much attendant jingoism. To cite only one case, an American propagandist journal, *The Navy*, carried in its issue of January 1914 a
plea to *Keep the flag flying.* The Flag "but a few years ago," it declared, with greater show of patriotic enthusiasm than of literary
elegance, "had blazed through the smoke above the guns of our
cruisers as they scorched the spirit of the Monroe Doctrine into the
heart of the Pacific seas and we planted in the Philippines the gage
of battle that yet may be the issue of a world-wide war, in which the
Ruling Race shall be swept from history or rise to its final supremacy. . . . Today that Flag, flying from the masthead of our free mer-
chantmen, is flaring its challenge to the subsidized ships of another
power [Japan] and beating them in the fight for trade and empire,
because the men who walk the quarterdecks of these big steam
galleons of ours are better men, in the large elemental way, than the
suave masters of the rival boats. . . . Our [merchantmen] have made
a path across the waters . . . that one day we may have to follow
with our troopships and our dreadnoughts, and in that day we will
be proud and thankful for the men who blazed the trail. *Hats off to
the Flag!*" World-wide war did come barely six months after publication of the article, and scarcely a generation later the Japanese
attack on Pearl Harbor swept the United States into World War II.

It is significant that during the forty years from 1874 to 1914
European arms and European materialism made a much greater impact on Asia and Africa than did Christianity, Europe's traditional
religion and the spiritual feature of its civilization. True, Christian
foreign missions, both Catholic and Protestant, spread and multiplied as never before in a like period of time; and besides making a
considerable number of converts in Africa, India, and the Far East,
they performed valuable service in providing schools, hospitals, and
medical care. Yet the converts they made were a small percentage

of the native population, and many Christian missionaries were more likely to reflect the European or American environment from which they came than to adapt themselves to the alien environment to which they went. Moreover, the behavior of many a European trader or soldier or administrator in "heathen" and "backward" lands was a handicap rather than a help to Christian missionaries.

Though countries and areas outside of historic Christendom were only marginally receptive to Christianity, and though they were inclined to cling tenaciously to their customary native religions, such as Hinduism, Confucianism, Buddhism, Shinto, Islam, or, as with African tribes, some form of primitive animism, they were immensely influenced in other ways by the national imperialism of Europe and America. The first and foremost example was Japan. Beginning in the 1860's, when American warships had opened it to Western contact and trade, Japan underwent an internal transformation, adopting the industrial, technical, material, and military features of European civilization and at the same time the intense nationalism of the era. Thereby Japan was enabled not only to ensure its national independence but by the 1890's to enter the characteristically European game of national imperialism and to take rank as a great power alongside the six in Europe and the United States in America.

Nationalism proved to be a major European export, with a constantly broadening market. Leading natives in India, China, Egypt, and elsewhere absorbed it through contact with resident Europeans—officials, traders, missionaries, schoolteachers—and still more through their attendance at colleges and universities in England, France, Germany, or the United States. And as native intellectuals became imbued with nationalist aspiration they communicated it to the masses. Both Mohandas Gandhi, the Hindu national leader and hero of his native India, and Mohammed Ali Jinnah, the Muslim founder and father of present-day Pakistan, were trained in law and admitted to the bar in England before 1914. Similarly, Dr. Sun Yat-sen, the venerated Chinese nationalist, obtained his early education in Hawaii and his medical training in British Hong Kong. And now the native leaders of newly created national states throughout "darkest Africa" are products also of European or American schooling.

Thus the imperialism which marked a flowering of European (and American) nationalism in the decades from 1870 to 1910, produced in time a fruitage of nationalist reactions among subject peoples everywhere. The results have become abundantly manifest since 1920 and most fatefully so since World War II.[1]

3. Intolerance Toward Religious Minorities

Contemporary with the new national imperialism was a manifold display of nationalist intolerance. Back of this was the drive of heated patriots for national strength and power, and their conviction that tolerance of dissent and division within a nation would gravely weaken it. Hence the entire population of a country should be trained and obliged to conform with the characteristics and beliefs of the major or dominant nationality. Minorities who didn't conform were suspect; they obviously lacked the requisite hundred per cent of national patriotism and therefore merited treatment as inferior, second-class citizens if not as downright traitors.

Among minorities which were objects of suspicion and compulsion, mention may be made of the religious. In Spain and Italy and in most of Latin America, where Catholicism was a national tradition and state religion, the individual might be agnostic and anticlerical and seldom if ever go to Mass, but he was not likely to turn Protestant and incur the stigma and the social and legal handicaps which acceptance of a "foreign" and "antinational" religion usually entailed.

Wherever Catholics were a minority, and even in traditionally Catholic countries where nationalist anticlericals were numerous and active, the Catholic Church was an object of attack. After all, Catholicism was much more of a supranational form of Christianity than either Protestantism or Eastern Orthodoxy. It was organized and disciplined under a nonnational pope. It had in Latin an official international language. It had a whole educational system of its own

[1] Illustrative material is provided by Bruce T. McCully's *English Education and Origins of Indian Nationalism* and Cyrus H. Peake's *Nationalism and Education in China*. See the comprehensive recent treatment of this important subject in Rupert Emerson's *From Empire to Nation* (1960), particularly pp. 197–209.

with schools, universities, seminaries, and Roman colleges. It had a habit of taking definite stands on matters of faith and morals. Small wonder that, in an age of intensifying nationalism, Catholics were accused of dividing their allegiance between nation and church and ultimately of obeying pope rather than national state. Liberals as well as Protestants and strenuous nationalists were greatly alarmed (quite unnecessarily, it has since turned out) by Pope Pius IX's *Syllabus of Errors* of 1864 with its apparent condemnation of "progress, liberalism, and modern civilization," and still more by the definition of papal infallibility at the Vatican Council in 1870.

In Germany Bismarck gave countenance during the 1870's and into the '80's to the so-called *Kulturkampf* ("battle of civilization") which the National Liberal and Radical parties waged against the Catholic Church. Relations with the papacy were broken off, Jesuits were banished, candidates for the priesthood were required to study at secular universities in Germany, and disobedience was made punishable by fines and imprisonment. For a time every German Catholic bishop was in jail or in exile, and in over 1,300 parishes Catholic worship ceased. Only the stubborn resistance of the Catholic laity, organized in the famous Center party and supported by a variety of other opponents of Bismarckian policies, stopped the *Kulturkampf.* Even so, however, the outcome was a truce rather than peace. Some of the anti-Catholic measures remained formally as German law until after World War I; and then anti-Catholic activity (and anti-Protestant also) was vigorously renewed by the mad Hitler and his furious Nazis. Catholic defense here, as elsewhere, was vindictively labeled "political Catholicism."

The Republican government of France encroached steadily, from 1879 to 1914, on the historic functions and liberties of the Catholic Church.[1] It did away with religious instruction in state schools and seriously handicapped church schools. It banned the Jesuit and other religious orders and congregations and expelled them from the country. In 1905 it abrogated Napoleon's concordat with the papacy,

[1] A judicious treatment of this during the decade from 1877 to 1889 will be found in Evelyn M. Acomb's *Laic Legislation in France.*

withdrew financial support from the clergy, and vested title to all church property in the state. Of supporters of these measures, some thought them needful for political reasons, others for intellectual or cultural ends, still others for social or economic purposes. Their foremost advocates were sterling patriots and nationalists—Gambetta, Ferry, Brisson, Combes, Viviani, Clemenceau.

In other traditionally Catholic countries, similar anticlerical nationalist movements were in evidence. As in France, so in Italy, in Spain, in Portugal, in Austria, and in the republics of Latin America, sometimes more and sometimes less, the Catholic Church was assailed. That this was aggravated in many cases by unreasonable intransigence or ultraconservatism of churchmen, admits of little doubt. That in large part it was both cause and effect of rising nationalism admits of no doubt. Of course in most so-called "Catholic countries," Catholicism was too much of a national tradition to be completely uprooted, and some of its adherents sought to identify it with their particular brand of nationalism and to make it serve their partisan politics. In the Russia of the Tsars, where Eastern Orthodoxy was the state and national religion, both Catholicism and Protestantism were regarded as foreign, the one "Polish" and the other "German," and as masks of "Western" liberalism and democracy; against them a series of discriminatory and persecuting decrees was promulgated.

In English-speaking countries, anti-Catholicism remained a conspicuous plank in the platform of a prevalent type of nationalism. It represented a deep and widespread popular feeling that Catholics, with their "divided allegiance," could not be thoroughly loyal citizens; and it was sustained and propagated, in the name of national patriotism, by professional agitators and publicists, and, in America, by a succession of organizations—"Know-Nothing party," "American Protective Association," "Ku Klux Klan," "Protestants and Others United," and so on. In fact the Catholic minority in Britain and in the United States did not lag behind their fellow citizens in the discharge of civic obligations or profession of national loyalty; they invariably bore at least their proportionate share of losses of blood and treasure in the wars of their respective nations. Yet just as Britishers thought it important to retain the legal prescription that their sovereign and some of his ministers must be "faithful Protestants," so a majority of Americans could be expected to oppose the election of a Catholic President.

4. Intolerance Toward "Racial" Minorities, Especially Jews

Nationalist intolerance in the era after 1870 was not only religious but racial. Earlier nationalists had frequently used the word "race," but in a loose way without pretense to scientific exactitude. Ever since Friedrich Schlegel, early in the nineteenth century, had delivered the dictum that there are as many races as there are languages, it had become commonplace to speak of a German race, a French race, a Slavic race, a Celtic race, an Anglo-Saxon race, and so on. This was, with most people, a merely conventional use of "race" as a synonym for nationality.

Racialism assumed a new and more sinister significance from the vogue of "social Darwinism," the extension to human affairs of Darwin's biological doctrine of the "struggle for existence and survival of the fittest," and its particular application to the national struggles of the 1860's and '70's. Clearly the nations that then "survived" and came off victorious were the "fittest." But what made a nation fittest? Drawing inspiration from Darwin's supplementary notion of the inheritance of acquired characteristics, certain scientists and pseudo-scientists—and nationalists—said it must be "blood," "heredity," "race."

The problem of finding out what the different human races were, and which were "fittest to survive," seemed soluble through a combination of two methods. One was to classify races, superior and inferior, according to mental and spiritual traits and then discover to which a man belonged by observing his behavior and measuring his intelligence. The other method was to classify races according to physical features. Combination of the methods appeared to confirm, "scientifically," that Germans, who had recently triumphed over France, belonged to a peculiarly valorous and superior race. Hence anyone who displayed "German" qualities of energy and bravery must belong to that race; and, conversely, anyone who, like the prevalent physical type of North German, was tall, blond, blue-eyed, and long-headed, must possess superior qualities of courage and intellect. This was quite consistent with, and reassuring to, German nationalism. And it was seized upon by a group of fanatical apostles, including Richard Wagner the musician, Adolf Wagner the economist, and Adolf Stöcker, court preacher. The last-named (how the name Adolf will recur!) exuberantly declared: "German blood flows in every German body, and the soul is in the blood. When one meets a German brother, and not merely a brother from common humanity, there is a certain reaction that does not occur if the brother is not German. Peoples can be compared to birds; there are different species."[1]

The Aryan myth—as such German racialism is properly described —was accepted and preached outside the German Empire. In France, for instance, it was expounded at length by the Comte de Gobineau, an aristocrat proud of the Germanic origins of his class and fearful of the leveling and corrupting influence of "inferior" races in his country, and likewise by Gustave Le Bon, a very opinionated and verbose "social psychologist." In the Habsburg Austrian Empire, Georg von Schönerer led a twofold movement in behalf of (1) bringing its "superior" German population into union with the Hohenzollern German Empire, and (2) cutting loose from the Catholic Church and adopting a German—and heroic—"racial Christianity." It is notable that the region of Austria most affected by Schönerer's movement[2] was the birthplace in 1889 of a long obscure Adolf Hitler, who developed in boyhood a passionate fondness for Wagner's nationalist music and Stöcker's racial demagoguery and was punished at school for singing, instead of the courtly *Kaiserlied,* the rousing *Deutschland über Alles.*

---

[1] Dietrich von Oertzen, *Adolf Stöcker, Lebensbild und Zeitgeschichte* (1912), pp. 260–261. For a devastating critique of "racialism," see Jacques Barzun's *Race, a Study in Modern Superstition* (1937).

[2] On Schönerer and Hitler's early intellectual environment, see William A. Jenks, *Vienna and the Young Hitler* (1960).

English and American publicists of presumably Anglo-Saxon lineage attributed the greatness of their countries to that stock—that superior Aryan and Teutonic race. Sir John Seeley in his *Expansion of England* (1883) proclaimed the British Empire to be the very embodiment of Anglo-Saxon superiority. To him and to numerous fellow imperialists, the motive force in all of England's greatness—political, commercial, industrial, and moral, no less than naval and colonial—was the "Anglo-Saxon race." And what easier explanation could be put forth of the growing strength and expansionist activity of the United States? "If I read not amiss," declared a Congregational clergyman of New England in 1885, "this powerful race will move down upon Mexico, down upon Central and South America, out upon the islands on the sea, over upon Africa and beyond. And can anyone doubt that the result of this competition of races will be the 'survival of the fittest' ?"[1]

Racialism gave new vigor and direction to anti-Jewish prejudice. Dislike of Jews and discrimination against them had long existed. They were everywhere a minority who preserved a good deal of clannishness and a good many traditions and customs different from the majority's. Christians were apt to dislike their religious recalcitrance; farmers, their urban-mindedness; conservatives, their flocking with liberals or Marxians. Yet at least in western and central Europe there had been a remarkable dwindling of anti-Jewish discrimination and prejudice in the first two-thirds of the nineteenth century and until the rise of racialism. Then anti-Jewish sentiment was rationalized and intensified as anti-Semitism. The Jews, it was now claimed, belonged to a Semitic *race* because the Hebrew spoken by their ancestors was a Semitic language, and their Semitic race couldn't help but transmit physical, mental, and moral traits different from the Aryan and irreconcilable with it. Hence there was no hope of changing Jewish habits and every reason for safeguarding Aryan nations against the degrading influence of Semitic minorities.

[1] Josiah Strong, *Our Country, Its Possible Future and Its Present Crisis.* See also the illuminating essay by E. N. Saveth, "Race and Nationalism in American Historiography: the Late 19th Century," *Political Science Quarterly,* LIV, 421–441 (September, 1939).

As Adolf Stöcker said, "The Jews are a nation within the nation, a state within a state, a race in the midst of another race. All other immigrants are ultimately assimilated in the nation where they live, but not the Jews. Their constant Semitism and their rigid ritual system and enmity to Christianity stand in direct contrast to the Germanic spirit."[1]

Stöcker, seconded by Adolf Wagner, organized an expressly anti-Semitic party in Germany in 1887; it polled 47,500 votes in 1890, and 285,000 eight years later. In Austria the German Nationalist party, founded by Schönerer in the early 1880's, was fanatically anti-Semitic as well as anti-Catholic. And from England came the son of a British admiral, Houston Stewart Chamberlain, who married Richard Wagner's daughter and settled in Germany, and whose writings were vehemently racialist and anti-Semitic.[2] In France, anti-Semitism was industriously preached by Edouard Drumont throughout the 1880's and '90's in books, pamphlets, and newspaper columns; it was an element in the nationalist movement that supported General Boulanger and a central factor in the notorious "Dreyfus affair."

In Russia the Tsar Alexander III (1881–1894), responding to anti-Semitic agitation, issued a series of oppressive decrees against Jews. Still worse, many government officials, taking their cue from the Tsar's attitude, gave free rein to anti-Jewish incitements to mob violence and tolerated, if they did not direct, those frightful anti-Jewish pogroms which were attended by plundering and burning and massacre. In the single year 1891 some 300,000 Jews fled the Russian Empire: it was the start of the high tide of Jewish migration to the United States.

5. Intolerance Toward Ethnic Minorities

While nationalist intolerance was displayed toward a supranational religion such as Catholic Christianity and toward a supposedly racial grouping such as Jews, its principal manifestation had to do

---

[1] Dietrich von Oertzen, *Adolf Stöcker,* p. 151.

[2] Epitomized in his *Foundations of the Nineteenth Century,* which was published in German in 1899 and in English translation in 1910.

with ethnic minorities. We should bear in mind that, despite the progress made since the French Revolution in redrawing the map of Europe along lines of nationality and in creating unified national states, no European state as yet embraced, or was confined to, a single nationality. Many German people were still outside the German Empire (chiefly in Austria, Switzerland, and Russia's Baltic provinces), while within it were Poles, Danes, and French-speaking Lorrainers. Italy lacked important "irredentas," and so did every one of the Balkan states. Belgium was bilingual, and Switzerland trilingual. Spain included Catalans and Basques as well as Castilians, and France a variety of "submerged" and "forgotten" peoples. Irish, Scots, and Welsh were joined with Englishmen in the "United Kingdom." Austria-Hungary and the Russian and Ottoman Empires, though dominated respectively by Germans and Magyars, by Russians, and by Turks, were not national states at all: they were polyglot and imperial.

This halting in the political sphere between a partially and an entirely nationalized Europe occurred when "the state" was assuming unprecedented functions and authority. It occurred likewise when doctrines and examples of forcefulness, racialism, and overseas imperialism were convincing dominant and "successful" nationalities that they were superior, and in duty bound to curb any agitation of "inferior" peoples for separate statehood and to keep them under the higher civilizing tutelage of the existing state. In other words, *raison d'état* compromised the working out of the principle of nationality. "National self-determination" gave way to "determination by superior peoples." Nationalism became imperialistic not only overseas but within Europe (and America).

Though of varying intensity in different countries, intolerance of ethnic minorities became common throughout Europe. In Scandinavia the Swedish regime most grudgingly made any concessions to Norwegian separatism. In Spain, both conservative and liberal statesmen combated autonomous movements of Catalans and Basques. The Third French Republic was adamant against any "regionalism" on the part of Bretons, Provençals, or Flemings, or the public use of any of their languages (which were belittled as *patois*). The half of Belgium's population which spoke French strove to Gallicize the half that spoke Flemish. In the Balkans, in manner *sui generis,* bands of Bulgarian, Serb, and Greek nationalists, frequently with the connivance of their respective governments, perpetrated rapine and murder in rival efforts to secure the allegiance of the Macedonian peasantry.

Englishmen, who usually sympathized with "oppressed" peoples on the Continent and their right to self-government, perceived slight justification for the exercise of any such right in Ireland. They deemed the Irish an inferior race, volatile, improvident, quarrelsome, backward, and Catholic, whose outbreaks, as in the Fenian outrages of the late 1860's and the Phoenix Park murders of the early '80's, had to be repressed with a strong arm. Besides, Ireland had in Ulster a "progressive" Protestant group that was decently faithful to Britain and the Empire and that must not be betrayed into the hands of a superstitious peasant majority. The British Parliament did gradually consent to some social and economic reforms in Ireland, but it rejected home-rule bills in 1886 and 1893, and in 1914 it deferred the execution of a third.

In 1886, just when Great Britain was denying home-rule to the Irish, the Prussian parliament was requesting Bismarck to speed up the "Germanization" of the three million Polish subjects. Bismarck willingly complied by announcing a twofold policy: Poles serving in the army or civil service "would be given an opportunity to avail themselves of the advantages of German civilization by being posted in German provinces far from their own homes"; and Polish landholdings would be bought up and distributed among German farmers pledged "to remain German and, above all, to marry German wives." Bismarck's retirement in 1890 interrupted anti-Polish legislation, but only temporarily. Through the propaganda efforts of a fiery group of German nationalists (the "HKT"), it was renewed and magnified from 1900 until World War I.[1] "Germanization" was also

[1] For details, see the illuminating study by Richard W. Tims, *Germanizing Prussian Poland: the HKT Society.*

directed against Danes in Schleswig and against French influence in Alsace-Lorraine. The latter territory remained under practically military rule; French was banished from the schools, and all autonomist protests were silenced.

"Russification" was a similar process. Its goal, as formulated and popularized by Slavophile nationalists was "one law [the Tsar's], one language [Great Russian], one religion [Russian Orthodox]." It began, in an important way, as an aftermath of the crushing of the Polish insurrection of 1863 and reached an advanced stage under Alexander III in the '80's. Every semblance of an autonomous Poland was obliterated, and in what had once been their country Poles were excluded from public office, obliged to use Russian in schools and law courts, and forbidden to sell land to anyone but a Russian. In Byelorussia and Lithuania, the Catholic population was coerced into employing the services of the Orthodox Church to legitimize marriage and children. In the Ukraine the native language was treated as a dialect and prohibited in printing, reciting, or singing. In the Baltic provinces, Russian was prescribed as the official tongue; the Protestant majority were forbidden to erect church buildings without consent of Orthodox authorities; and German place names were changed to Russian. Even Finland was deprived by the Tsar Nicholas II of the autonomy which his predecessors had guaranteed and usually respected. The harsh anti-Jewish decrees of the time were part of the same "Russification."

In the Austrian half of the Habsburg Empire, German nationalists championed the maintenance of traditional German hegemony, although the subject peoples, especially Poles and Czechs, were too numerous and too well organized to admit of any such sustained "Germanization" as Prussia directed against its Poles. On the other hand, the Hungarian half of the Empire was subjected by its historically ruling nationality (a minority of the country's total population) to drastic "Magyarization." The self-government previously accorded to the Croats was sharply abridged, and use of the Magyar language was made compulsory in schools and courts there and likewise in regions peopled by Serbs, Slovaks, and Rumanians.

There was also a simultaneous outburst of "Americanization" in the United States, a stirring and speeding up of the "melting pot," in order to produce from varied European strains a single and superior nationality. And in the first decade of the twentieth century a "Turk-ification" emerged and wrought havoc in the Ottoman Empire. To this we shall revert in the next chapter.

6. Nationalist Reaction of Subject Peoples

Nationalism among subject peoples of Europe was not lessened or quieted by repressive measures such as those just indicated. Rather, it was stimulated and intensified. In Spain, Basques and Catalans fought for national autonomy in the civil war of the 1870's (and again, more fiercely, in the civil war of the 1930's). In the late '70's, propaganda was extended for a Provençal literary revival through the French regions of Provence, Languedoc, and Aquitaine; in the '90's the propaganda turned political with demand for "Provençal autonomy within a federalized France." The demand was echoed by exponents of other regionalisms—Breton, Flemish, Corsican, and Basque—who, however, were more voluble than numerous and whose prime loyalty was unquestionably to France. In Belgium, Flemish nationalism passed in the '80's from cultural to political, from intellectuals to the compact masses of the northern and western districts; it eventually forced the Parliament at Brussels to make Flemish, equally with French, an official language of the state.

Irish nationalism entered a new phase in the late 1870's with Parnell's organization of a Nationalist party which returned to the British House of Commons four-fifths of all Irish members, and with Michael Davitt's founding of a Land League which enlisted the bulk of Irish peasants in the cause of agrarian reforms. Neither Land League nor Nationalist politicians employed conventional methods of the kid-glove kind. While the one incited to acts of violence against objectionable landlords, the other made trouble for the British Parliament by heckling speakers, obstructing procedure, and hurling inkstands. Some land reform was forthcoming, though the Nationalist party failed to get "home rule" for Ireland. This failure, nevertheless, spurred other nationalist activity. In the 1890's a Gaelic League was inaugurated by Douglas Hyde for the preservation and restoration of Gaelic, the historic national language; the famous Abbey Theatre was opened at Dublin for the presentation of Irish plays; a cooperative movement for national economic betterment was launched by Sir Horace Plunkett. Most portentous was the return from South Africa, at the close of the decade, of a journalist, Arthur Griffith, with the burning conviction that Ireland should not beg home rule or anything else of a "foreign" British Parliament, but should follow a policy of *sinn fein,* that is, it should rely on itself and its own powers of passive resistance to achieve full national statehood. And from the United States came a youth, Eamon De Valera, half-Spanish, half-Irish, who in course of time was to be Griffith's able lieutenant and successor.

Czech nationalism ran a course similar to Irish. The Czechs, who constituted a majority of the population of the Austrian provinces of Bohemia and Moravia, resented the denial to them of the national autonomy accorded in 1867 to Hungary, and in the 1880's and '90's they backed a political party whose representatives in the Austrian Parliament adopted the disorderly methods of contemporary Irish Nationalists. In fact the Austrian Parliament fared worse than the British, for Czech obstructionists were abetted by deputies of other disgruntled nationalities—Slovenes, Italians, Ukrainians (Ruthenians), and Rumanians. Bad matters were made worse by the democratic electoral reform of 1907, which introduced universal and compulsory manhood suffrage, thereby giving the non-German nationalities of Austria a preponderence over the German.[1] Henceforth the conflicts and disorders in the conduct of parliamentary government at Vienna were so magnified as to render it practically inoperative and to bring about its supplanting by what amounted to governmental dictatorship and martial law. By this time, Czech nationalists, despairing of obtaining home rule from the Austrian Emperor or Parliament, were finding and following more radical leaders, such as Professor Tomáš Masaryk, who advocated common

[1] Pertinent is William A. Jenks's *Austrian Electoral Law of 1907.*

action of Hungarian Slovaks with Austrian Czechs in the building, if necessary by war and with Russian aid, of a free and united Czechoslovakia.

Similar reaction of the subject nationalities of Hungary was less in the limelight at the time, mainly because they were very slightly represented, and hence comparatively silenced, in the undemocratic Parliament at Budapest. This is not to say, however, that they acquiesced in the Magyarization which was visited upon them and which was actually more repressive than anything endured by the Czechs. On the contrary, the bulk of the Croat, Serb, Slovak, and Rumanian peoples in Hungary were now more determined than ever to cling to their respective languages and traditions and more ready to accept the leadership of extremists.

Poles, distributed among the three great powers of Russia, Germany, and Austria, were in a peculiarly difficult position. They were intensely patriotic, and few were without the dream of a gloriously resurrected and reunited Polish state. Yet they differed as to how the dream might be realized. One group, rapidly diminishing in the presence of current "Russification," looked to Russia or Pan-Slavism; another, to the Germanic powers, more to Austria than to Prussian Germany where "Germanization" was rife; while a third and growing number, skeptical about the early appearance of any messiah, urged self-reliance, a stimulated solidarity among Russian, Prussian, and Austrian Poles, and a vigorous campaign in defense of common national culture and economy and in behalf of provincial autonomy.

Norwegians, too, nourished a nationalism both cultural and political. On one hand, as their literary and official language they supplemented or substituted for the Danish speech (*riksmaal*) of the cities a more or less artificial synthesis of indigenous rural dialects (*landsmaal*). On the other hand they pressed Sweden, with which they had been forcibly united in 1814, for an ever larger degree of self-government, until at last in 1905 they succeeded in separating themselves from Sweden and setting up a completely independent national state.

Subject peoples in the Russian Empire, especially those along its western borders, reacted against "Russification" by evincing or intensifying some type of counternationalism—cultural, or political, or both. Mention has already been made of the Poles. A similar nationalism possessed Finns, and, to only lesser degree, Lithuanians and Letts, Ukrainians (Little Russians, or Ruthenians) and Byelorussians (White Russians). All these peoples tended to sympathize with the revolutionary movement which overspread the Russian Empire in 1905–1906, and their nationalist leaders were active in it. Although the movement was curbed in most respects, there was slackening of "Russification," and Finland actually regained a measure of self-government.

We should not overlook, in this connection, the nationalistic reaction of Jews to the era's anti-Semitism. Many of them, stung by imputations against their "racial" character, became acutely race-conscious and, in a sense, exemplars of racialism; at least they were inclined to sink religious and cultural differences in an assumed ethnic unity. Stung also by nationalist taunts that they were "aliens" and could not be loyal patriotic citizens of countries where they lived, they tended, in defense or as compensation, to develop a Jewish nationalism.[1] In 1896 a Hungarian Jew, Theodor Herzl, came forward with principles and a program for just such nationalism. "Zionism," he called it. To him, Jews were really and truly a distinctive nationality, with a language, a culture, and historical traditions peculiar to themselves; they should therefore have an independent national state, preferably in Palestine. The next year the first general congress of Zionists was held at Basel, and soon the movement enlisted an enthusiastic following among Jews in many lands.

[1] For an understanding of Jewish nationalism as a religion, divorced from Biblical and historic Judaism, see the convenient collection of translated writings of *Simon Dubnow*, ed. by Koppel Pinson (1958).

CHAPTER IX

Nationalism, Cause and Result of World War I

I. National Versus Imperial States in Eastern Europe

By the start of the present century, progress had been made in redrawing the political map of Europe along lines of nationality. In addition to the older national states on the Atlantic seaboard, there were now national states in central Europe for Italians and Germans and in the southeast for Greeks, Serbs, Rumanians, and Bulgarians. In other words, national states had become the prevalent form of government throughout full half of the Continent. These, as I have pointed out in the preceding chapter, might not include the whole of a nationality, and in fact they might contain some dissentient national minorities, but each had as its core and dominant majority a people with distinctive speech and traditions.

The situation in most of eastern Europe was different and equivocal. Here were a large number of nationalities, with intensifying cultural nationalism, but without national states of their own and subjected to one or another of three surviving empires—the Russian, the Ottoman, or the Austrian. The Russian Empire was an approximation to the national states of western Europe in that a single nationality (the "Great Russian") constituted a majority of its inhabitants and shared a common patriotism. Nevertheless its subject nationalities, especially those in the Empire's western provinces and in the Caucasus, resented the "Russification" applied by the Tsar's government, and their leaders could be counted upon to sympathize and cooperate with revolutionary movements aimed against the autocratic imperial regime.

The Austrian Empire, or, as it was now officially called, the Dual Monarchy of Austria-Hungary, was an outstanding example, in east-central Europe, of the imperial, nonnational state. It contained a hodgepodge of nationalities. Since 1867 Germans and Magyars jointly exercised predominance, the one in the Austrian half of the Empire and the other in the Hungarian half. Subservient in Austria were Czechs, Poles, Ruthenians (Ukrainians), Slovenes, and some Rumanians and Italians; in Hungary, similarly, were Slovaks, Croatians, Serbs, and Rumanians. Together, these subject peoples outnumbered Germans and Magyars combined, and their majority was further enlarged by the Empire's military occupation in 1878 of the Ottoman provinces of Bosnia-Herzegovina, peopled by Serbs, and their formal annexation in 1908. Each of the Empire's numerous peoples had come to cherish a distinctive cultural nationalism, which was now supplemented and fortified by some degree of political nationalism. In the circumstances it seemed inevitable that sooner or later the Empire must disintegrate and be replaced, as in western Europe, by a congeries of national states.

The Empire survived, nevertheless, well into the twentieth century, and it did so without altering its basic character. Indeed, it continued to appear strong, retaining position and prestige as one of the six great powers of Europe; and neither "Germanization" nor the stiffer and more intolerant "Magyarization," though resented, brought any open rebellion. For an understanding of this paradoxical situation, we may recall that the Austrian Empire represented a continuation of the ancient Roman Empire, and as such a political and cultural entity much older than any existing national state and one imbuing subjects, as well as rulers, with a conservatism associated with historic army, church, and *mores*. Its various peoples might be stirred by modern nationalism, but in general, prior to 1914, they conservatively sought its political attainment through self-government within a reformed federal Empire rather than through the Empire's destruction. Some of their leaders may also have appreciated the economic advantage of a large, internally free-trade empire over a group of small, competitive and tariff-walled national states. There certainly was, throughout Austria-Hungary, a widespread personal loyalty to the seemingly ageless Emperor Francis Joseph, whose reign had already lasted over half a century. At least as long as he lived, the Austrian Empire was likely to last.

The Ottoman Empire, on the contrary, had been for some time in actual and obvious process of disintegration. It had failed to keep pace with other European countries in industrial development and armed strength; and during the nineteenth century most of its African possessions had broken loose and been appropriated by France or Britain, while it had been deprived of a large part of its European provinces through foreign war and internal rebellion and resulting creation of national states for Greeks, Rumanians, Serbs, and Bulgarians.

In vain Turkish nationalists attempted revolutionary reforms in 1908–1909, including "Turkification" of subject peoples remaining within the Empire. After all, however, the Turks comprised a minority of the population of the Ottoman Empire, and their newly asserted and intolerant nationalism simply threw the Empire into turmoil and made bad matters worse. It met resistance even in the Asiatic provinces, not only from Christian Armenians but from Muslim Arabs and Kurds. In Europe, it afforded opportunity for Austria-Hungary definitely to annex Bosnia-Herzegovina, and for Bulgaria to sever its last nominal ties with the Empire. It especially stimulated counternationalism among the Serb, Greek, and Bulgarian inhabitants of Ottoman Macedonia, and aroused it among the hitherto comparatively quiescent Albanians. Most significantly, Greece and the Balkan states were filled with crusading zeal in behalf of their fellow nationals within the Empire.

The chain of events leading immediately to World War I began with the Ottoman Empire's defeat by imperialistic Italy in 1911–1912 and its resulting loss of Libya in North Africa and of the Greek-speaking Dodecanese Islands in the Aegean. This showed how vulnerable Turkish defense really was, and how possible it would be for Greece and the Balkan states, if they pooled their resources and acted together, to "free" their kinsmen and end Turkish rule in Europe. The international situation appeared auspicious. Russia was traditionally favorable to them; and with Russia, France was allied and Great Britain friendly. On the other side, Germany, which had latterly posed as friend and patron of the Turks, was now embarrassed by the recent aggressions of its allies, Austria-Hungary and Italy, against the Ottoman Empire, and hence was inclined to back it more by diplomatic than by direct military means.

So in spite of mutual jealousies and conflicting ambitions, leaders of the national states bordering on the Ottoman Empire in Europe —the wily King Ferdinand of Bulgaria, the passionately patriotic King Peter and Prime Minister Pašić of Serbia, and the astute Prime Minister Venizelos of Greece—agreed, just before the end of the Italo-Turkish War, to make joint attack on the Empire and to divide the spoils among themselves. The ensuing Balkan War of 1912 was a triumph for the national allies. Their armies overran Macedonia, and the Bulgarian army got within sight of Constantinople. But a peace settlement was harder to attain. Austria-Hungary, fearful of the effect of an enlarged and triumphant Serbia on its own Serbs, threatened to intervene unless the share of the Ottoman spoils marked out for Serbia in western Macedonia, and in the vicinity of Bosnia, was drastically reduced. Serbia very reluctantly consented, but demanded as compensation part of the share tentatively allotted to Bulgaria.

Bulgaria refused, and what is known as the Second Balkan War quickly ensued in 1913, with Serbia, Greece, the Ottoman Empire, and now Rumania also, arrayed against Bulgaria. Thereby the Empire was enabled to retain Constantinople, the Straits, and a small bordering area in Europe, though it lost all Macedonia and most of Thrace, and was henceforth confined principally to Asia. Bulgaria, while retaining a portion of its previous conquests, had to make cessions to its former allies and to Rumania. Albania emerged as an independent national state. Both Greece and Serbia acquired national extension and unification at the expense of the Ottoman Empire. Venizelos was hailed as the Cavour of Greece; Pašić and King Peter as respectively the Bismarck and William I of Serbia.

Particularly in the case of Serbia, the two Balkan Wars of 1912–1913 served to whet, rather than to appease, nationalist ambition. ▸True, they had brought about the emancipation of all Serbs from the Ottoman Empire and had so weakened that Empire as to portend its early demise. But that was only half the task ahead for nationalistic Serbia. There remained the Austrian Empire, containing as many subject Serbs (with kindred Croats and Slovenes) as there had been in the Ottoman Empire. They too must be emancipated and unified with Serbia. And the anti-Serbian attitude and policy exhibited by Austria-Hungary during the Balkan Wars fed the flame of Serbian nationalism.

The issue was clearly between an older empire and a newer national state. Could an imperial state survive in Europe, or would it succumb in eastern Europe, as it had in the West, to national states? National states had just won out against the Ottoman Empire. The next and decisive test would be between a national state and the Habsburg Empire of Austria-Hungary. And this would precipitate World War I, the greatest and most destructive war up to that time in all recorded history.

2. *Nationalism in the War* (*1914–1918*)

On June 28, 1914, at Sarajevo, the capital city of Bosnia, the heir to the imperial throne of Austria-Hungary was assassinated by a fanatical young Serb nationalist. The government at Vienna, which had been restrained by its German ally from attacking Serbia during the Balkan Wars, now utilized the gasp of horror which followed the assassination in order to obtain from William II and his Chancellor at Berlin an assurance that Germany would support it in any action it might take against Serbia. Then it dispatched an ultimatum to Belgrade, accusing Serbia of complicity in the crime and demanding acceptance of the Empire's control of nationalist propaganda and conduct from within Serbia. Serbia, abetted by Russia, temporized. Austria-Hungary, insisting that its very existence was at stake, declared war against Serbia on July 28, 1914. The crucial test between empire and national state was at hand.

If the test could have been simply one between imperial Austria-Hungary and nationalist Serbia, it would probably have issued in victory and enhanced prestige for the former, and an indefinite post-ponement of the political nationalizing of east-central Europe. But what began as a localized war turned speedily into a vast general war of which nationalism was the major motivating force. The Russian government of the Tsar, actuated by Pan-Slavic opposition to Austria-Hungary and by nationalist ambition to play the role of big brother and guardian of Slavic peoples in general and Serbs in par-ticular, kept its pledge of support to Serbia by ordering partial, then general, mobilization (July 29–30). Now that Russian participation in the war appeared certain, the German government felt obliged to honor the assurance it had given to Austria-Hungary, which, with its ruling Germans and Magyars, was Germany's one dependable great-power ally. If the Austrian Empire should fall prey to Slavic conquest, it was reasoned, Germany and the German nationality were sure to suffer. So a German ultimatum was dispatched to Russia (July 31), demanding cessation of military preparations along the border. No reply was forthcoming. On August 1, Germany declared war against the Russian Empire.

In expectation that France, the ally of Russia, would seize the op-portunity to attempt recovery of the "lost" provinces of Alsace-Lor-raine, Germany promptly delivered at Paris an ultimatum requiring guarantees of French neutrality. The answer was that France would "consult her own interests." Thus it transpired that on August 3 Germany also declared war on France, and German armies were set in motion through Luxembourg and Belgium on the way to France. Until then the uncertain attitude of the British government had en-couraged German hopes for Great Britain's neutrality, but on August 4, as a result of German violation of Belgian neutrality, not only the Belgian but the British government declared war on Germany.

All the European great powers, except Italy, were accordingly at war within ten days of its outbreak between Austria-Hungary and

Serbia, and Italy joined within the next ten months. Eventually all European countries, small as well as large, were at war, except the Scandinavian, the Netherlands, Switzerland, and Spain. Eventually at war, too, were the overseas British Commonwealth (and India), Japan, the Ottoman Empire, the United States, China, and, at least nominally, a number of other nations in the Americas, Asia, and Africa.

We need not here rehearse the epic story of World War I. It lasted over four years and turned out to be a supremely nationalistic war. On one side was the mighty effort of the national Hohenzollern Empire not only to retain its earlier conquests and subject peoples, and to extend itself against "inferior" neighbors, but also to safeguard German-Magyar rule in the Austrian Empire, and Turkish in the Ottoman, and to help Bulgaria avenge its defeat in the previous Balkan war. On the opposing side, against those four "Central Powers" were the other belligerents—the "Allies"—motivated by considerations of national defense or national expansion or national prestige.

As soon as war was declared, both masses and classes rallied to the support of their respective governments. Earlier professions of pacifism or neutrality quickly evaporated, and failure marked the movements and organizations which, it had been imagined, might check, if not exorcise, the war spirit. Christianity failed: no heed was given to pacific pleas of anguished pope or other priests and ministers. Marxian socialism failed: its following made no attempt to stay or impede the war by "general strike" or any other means. "Intellectuals" failed: the large majority of them deserted reason for emotion, fair-mindedness for bellicose partnership. So, too, failed "big business" and "international finance," and other economic considerations, which publicists such as Norman Angell had prophesied would militate against, and prevent, the enormous cost and ultimate universal bankruptcy that large-scale modern warfare would entail.

The war spirit was too strong, too irresistible. It swept like a forest fire or prairie dust storm. The way for it had been prepared by the industrialization and materialism, the international rivalries and competitive imperialism of the era since 1870, and the attendant myths about "superior" races and peoples, about "the struggle for existence and survival of the fittest." Moreover, and this is the most important explanation of general surrender to the war, the masses in industrialized Europe, America, and Japan were now thoroughly imbued with nationalism through popular schooling and popular journalism. Thereby, nationalist propaganda, directed by the several national states, proved extraordinarily effective in silencing criticism of one's own country and instilling hate of the enemy. This was attested, for example, by the practical unanimity with which Britishers dubbed the Germans "Huns" and accused them of cutting off the hands of Belgian children. And woe to any foreigner who might be found in a country with which his own country was at war. He could experience no such liberty and hospitality as, back in the eighteenth century, a Voltaire had enjoyed in England, or a Gibbon in France, while their nations were at war with each other. He was now regarded as a spy, real or potential, and duly interned or put under surveillance. War was now truly totalitarian. It was mass war.

Thanks to ascendant popular nationalism, there was general unquestioning acceptance of mobilization and the draft, of press censorship, and of virtual state socialism through governmental regulation and operation of transportation, munitions manufacture, food rationing, and banking. All this had been foreshadowed a century earlier by Revolutionary and Napoleonic France, but that was at an early stage of modern nationalism on the European Continent and it was then exemplified primarily by Frenchmen, and not nearly so completely even by them. Now, a century later, the nationalism which had inspired French *Jacobins* and Napoleon's *Grande Armée* was common mass possession of most of Europe and far beyond.

Any subject nationality which showed signs of revolt or insubordination was sternly repressed. Those in Austria-Hungary were kept in order for over three years by the military authorities of the Empire, assisted by those of Germany. An Irish Republican uprising at Dublin at Eastertime of 1916 was quickly put down by British troops and its captured leaders were put to death. On the other hand, belligerent states fostered nationalism wherever it might be helpful to themselves and hurtful to their enemies. For instance, Great Britain, bent on overwhelming the Ottoman Empire, promised the nationalistic Zionists, through the Balfour Declaration of 1917, a future Jewish "homeland" in Palestine, while at the same time permitting Captain Lawrence to make similar, and in part contradictory, promises to the Arabs. The Allies likewise obtained cooperation of Italy and Rumania against the Austrian Empire by assuring them, as well as Serbia, that they might share liberally in the Empire's partition. As counterweights, Germany backed Bulgarian nationalism against Serbian and Rumanian; and jointly with Austria-Hungary, Germany vied with Russia in holding out to the Poles the prospect of some sort of national resurrection.

3. The Peace of Paris and Triumph of Nationalism Throughout Europe

The war lasted longer than had been expected at the outset; and it was a tribute to the arms production of industrialized national states, and particularly to the mass nationalism of their citizens, that all such states, despite terrifying losses of men and property, persevered in the war to the very end. The Russian Empire was the first to quit. It lagged behind western and central Europe in industrial development and the manufacture of munitions. Its subject nationalities were restless and undependable. Its government was corrupt and inefficient. Its armies, being largely illiterate, were heedless of war propaganda and apparently willing to follow any party or leader that would bring peace. This was attained by Lenin's small but highly disciplined Bolshevik Communist party which wrought the revolution of November, 1917, and then capitulated to Germany.

For another year, Germany, fighting furiously, was able to launch one offensive after another against the remaining Allies, and thereby to bolster temporarily its hard-pressed war companions—the Austrian and Ottoman Empires and Bulgaria. By November, 1918, however, Germany could no longer withstand its foes, now joined in overwhelming force by the United States. Bulgaria and the Ottoman

Empire, hemmed in by foreign enemies and upset by domestic revolution, had already surrendered. Imperial Austria-Hungary, barely surviving the death of the venerable Emperor Francis Joseph, was now disowning his Habsburg successor, the Emperor Charles, and breaking up along lines of its component nationalities. In sum, World War I ended with the triumph not only of Serbia over Austria-Hungary, but, throughout Europe, of nationalism over historic imperialism, of national over imperial states.

The Paris Peace Congress of 1919–1920, unlike the Vienna Congress of 1815, recognized the principle of nationality and wrote it into the public law of Europe. At last the political map of the entire Continent was radically revised and redrawn. Four great imperial domains were dismembered—the Dual Monarchy of Austria-Hungary, the Ottoman Empire, the Russian Empire, the German Empire. Certain small states or provinces, whose inhabitants comprised but a fraction of a nationality, lost their historic identity and names—for example, Bohemia, Transylvania, Schleswig—and were incorporated with areas peopled by the same linguistic nationality. Thus six independent national states were newly created or restored: Poland, Czechoslovakia, Lithuania, Latvia, Estonia, and Finland. Six others were enlarged and consolidated: Serbia (as Yugoslavia), Rumania, Greece, Italy, France (by recovering Alsace-Lorraine), and Denmark (by obtaining northern Schleswig). Four states which had previously been imperial were so compressed as to consist of a single nationality: Germany, German Austria, Magyar Hungary, and Turkey.

The Russian Communists, though not participating in the Paris Peace Congress, seemed to agree with it in recognizing the principle of nationality. They consented, reluctantly and under some duress, to the secession from the Empire of the Baltic states (including Poland and Finland) and the annexation of Bessarabia by Rumania. And under the guidance of Lenin's "Commissar of Nationalities," Joseph Stalin, himself not a Russian but a Georgian from the Caucasus, the extensive remainder of the Russian Empire was reorganized as a nationally federated Soviet Socialist Union. Much the largest part

—the part peopled by the "Great Russian" nationality—became the "Russian Soviet Socialist Republic," with its capital at Moscow. Other parts were constituted Soviet Socialist Republics respectively for Ukrainians ("Little Russians"), Byelorussians ("White Russians"), Georgians, Armenians, and various tribal peoples in Turkestan and Siberia. All of these were subject, of course, to rigid control by the centralized Communist party and dictatorship, but each was freed from "Russification" of the Tsarist type and accorded a degree of cultural nationalism.

To recast the political map of eastern and central Europe on a strictly national basis was extraordinarily difficult, if not impossible. There had been, in the previously imperial and nonnational domains, much intermingling of peoples, with the result that now every newly erected or enlarged national state contained, besides a majority nationality, a considerable number of persons of dissident nationality. To be sure, boundaries were determined in a few instances by plebiscite. That was the case in Schleswig between Germany and Denmark, in East Prussia between Germany and Poland, in the Saar between Germany and France. Such plebiscites, however, did not get rid of the problem of national minorities, a problem which was aggravated by the drawing of boundaries by victors in the World War so as to penalize their enemies. Thus, all non-Germans were severed from Germany and Austria, all non-Magyars from Hungary, all non-Bulgarians from Bulgaria, and almost all non-Turks from Turkey. But simultaneously, sizable German minorities passed under the sway of Poland, Czechoslovakia, and Italy; Magyar minorities under the rule of Czechoslovakia, Rumania, and Yugoslavia; Bulgarian minorities under the dominion of Yugoslavia, Rumania, and Greece. Contrary to the principle of nationality, German Austria was prohibited from uniting with Germany.

Moreover, the arbitrariness with which frontiers were delimited between some of the national states—for example between Italy and Yugoslavia—tended to accentuate, rather than to allay, nationalist friction. Actual fighting over frontiers occurred as an aftermath of World War I between Poland and Lithuania and between Greece and Turkey. Nor was friction eased, or nationalism assuaged, by the treaty pledges extorted at Paris from freed or enlarged states, such as Poland and Rumania, that they would accord special rights to national minorities.

Each of the new national states aspired, like the older ones on the Continent, to self-sufficiency in all things. They all pursued from the outset policies of economic nationalism, especially the erection of tariff barriers against their neighbors. This, together with regulated new currencies and with restrictions on migration, was apt to be really uneconomic and to retard recovery from war losses. It was particularly so in the supplanting of a fairly large area of common free markets, such as imperial Austria-Hungary had been, by a group of comparatively small but economically isolated, national states. Here, as elsewhere, was clear evidence of the primacy of nationalistic over economic considerations.

Woodrow Wilson, great idealist and leading architect of the peace settlement of 1919–1920, earnestly believed and eloquently contended that putting Europe, and ultimately the world, on a national basis would serve to ensure lasting peace—*if* the several peoples had democratic institutions, and *if* they were joined in "a general association of nations . . . under specific covenants for the purpose of affording guarantees of political independence and territorial integrity." To the American President, this last of his famous Fourteen Points was not the least.

A confederation of the nations of the world, Wilson reiterated, would be "the most essential part of the peace settlement." He insisted upon its unqualified acceptance by the Allies and by Germany as a condition of the armistice of November, 1918, and from the ensuing negotiations at Paris he did get a "Covenant" for a "League of Nations." He was convinced that nationalism must be tempered with internationalism, and particularly that a League of Nations was essential for future peaceful correction of whatever imperfections or injustices there might be in the current settlement. Woodrow Wilson had the satisfaction of formally inaugurating the League in January 1920. It proved to be for him a sole and tragic satisfaction.

For the President encountered in his own country a storm of isolating nationalism whipped up in the wake of World War I. There was strenuous opposition to the League of Nations as tending to impair American sovereignty, to violate the American Constitution, and, in disregard of the counsels of George Washington, to entangle the United States in the meshes of Old World rivalry. The United States Senate stubbornly refused to ratify the League Covenant without drastic reservations which the President, with equal stubbornness, rejected. In vain the President appealed to the American people. They failed him and elected as his successor the somewhat earthy and provincial Warren Harding, who proclaimed in characteristically pompous style that "in the existing League of Nations, world governing with its super-powers, this Republic will have no part."

The abstention and critical attitude of the United States gravely damaged the League of Nations. But there was other nationalist obstruction to the League's successful operation. Continuing hostility of Allied peoples toward Germany, even though it was now a dismembered, disarmed, and democratic Republic, delayed its admission to the League of Nations and militated against any sane solution of the problem of war reparations and debts or any fulfillment of the promise of general disarmament. The League, in fact, turned out to be primarily an agency of France and Great Britain, and their respective satellites; and national distrust and rivalry, which was soon manifest between the principals, added to the League's ineffectualness. It could not ensure international peace or prevent aggression in turn by Japan, Italy, Germany, and Russia. Within a score of years it fell victim to World War II and collapsed utterly.

Meanwhile, the nationalism so evident in World War I and in the Paris peace settlement affected several small and "submerged" peoples of western Europe. In Belgium the Flemish-speaking population showed resentment against their French-speaking countrymen, some going so far as to demand political autonomy or even independence; and after the war the government conceded equality of the Flemish language with French and the transformation of the University of Ghent into a purely Flemish institution. In Spain there was a marked recrudescence of nationalism among Catalans and Basques, which led to the revolutionary Republic's granting them a large measure of autonomy that was forcefully annulled, however, under the subsequent dictatorship of General Franco. In Iceland, a burst of popular nationalism impelled Denmark to recognize its old colony as a new sovereign state. Even the Swiss Confederation displayed signs of linguistic nationalism during the war: its German-speaking cantons evinced partiality toward Germany; its French-speaking and Italian-speaking cantons, toward France and Italy respectively.

In Ireland nationalism was quickened by Britain's bloody suppression of the Easter Rebellion of 1916. In the next general election (December, 1918), three-fourths of all Irish constituencies were carried by Sinn Fein candidates, who, instead of taking their seats in the British Parliament at Westminster, met at Dublin and declared themselves the legal Parliament (or *Dail*) of the Irish Republic, with DeValera as President and Griffith as Vice President.[1] For three years a desultory but desperate struggle ensued. The British government sought vainly to "restore order," but it succeeded only in detaching from the island's thirty-two counties the six in Ulster where Unionists had a majority, and in setting up there a dependent "home-rule" government of "Northern Ireland." At length, by a treaty signed at London in December 1921, Britain agreed to the establishment of an "Irish Free State," embracing most of Ireland and constituting a self-governing Dominion similar in status to Canada. Eventually, we know, the Free State cut all political ties with the British Empire and became an independent national state. And in true nationalistic fashion, it prescribed school instruction in Gaelic, the old native language.

4. Stimulus to Nationalism Outside Europe

Nationalism could not be so aroused in belligerent countries during World War I, or so applied to the postwar territorial settlement in

[1] See above, p. 113.

Europe, without affecting the world at large. This was shown by America's relapse into isolation and by the stiffened restrictions it placed on foreign immigration. It was also exhibited by the self-governing Dominions of the British Empire: Canada, Australia, New Zealand, and South Africa. Each of these was newly stirred by pride in its military exploits during the war, by faith in its increasing future importance, and by determination to have its voice heard in the counsels of the world not indirectly through London but directly through its own national capital. Each signed the peace treaties of Paris as a sovereign power, and each was admitted to separate membership in the League of Nations. By the "Statute of Westminster" of December, 1931, they were legally transformed from dependency on Great Britain into an alliance of independent states officially styled the "British Commonwealth."

Outside the British Commonwealth, whose preponderant population was of European stock, the overseas imperialism of European nations that had characterized the preceding era seemed at first glance to be only slightly affected by World War I. To be sure, defeated Germany was shorn by the peace settlement of all its colonial possessions, but these as well as Asian territory detached from the Ottoman Empire were merely distributed, under the euphemistic title of "mandates," among victorious powers, mainly Britain, France, and Japan.

Yet actually there were postwar nationalistic developments among supposedly "colonial" and "backward" peoples which boded ill for the permanence of European imperial sway. An early and striking example was furnished by major Muslim nationalities of the Near and Middle East: Turks, Persians, and Arabs. The Turks, under the leadership of a patriotic army officer and dictator, Mustafa Kemal, took advantage of rivalries and war-weariness among the Allies to nullify the treaty which had been imposed by them upon the Ottoman Empire and which had awarded areas in Asia Minor to Greece and, as "mandates," to France and Italy. By fighting and diplomacy, Mustafa wrung from Greece and the Allies in 1923 a revised treaty, assuring the freedom and unity of all ethnically Turkish lands—the whole of Anatolia and Asia Minor and the European district of Constantinople.[1]

Turkey as thus constituted was only a portion of the former Ottoman Empire, but it was an important portion and it was now a truly national state. Moreover, an interesting, though painful, nationalist novelty of the settlement between Turkey and Greece was the enforced interchange of people. Many thousands of Christian Greeks were uprooted from ancient ancestral homes in seaports of Asia Minor and transplanted to Greece, while their places were taken by Muslim Turks who had lived on the Greek islands or mainland. Cyprus, for a time under British rule, was an exception, continuing to harbor troublously the two nationalities of Greek and Turk.

Under Mustafa Kemal's guidance, Turkey was rapidly nationalized. Not only was the imperial Sultanate ended, but Turkish institutions were pried loose from historic Islam and endowed with a secular and national character. Government appropriations for religion were suppressed, and religious schools were replaced by state schools. The old legal system, which had been based on the Koran and decisions of Muslim judges, was superseded by a modern national system. The West European calendar was substituted for the Muslim, and the Roman alphabet for the Arabic. Fez and turban were outlawed in favor of hats and caps. Women were forbidden to wear veils. The people were ordered to adopt surnames (Kemal himself took the surname of "Atatürk"—"Chief Turk"). Most Turks continued to be Muslims, but Islam was henceforth a private and not a public concern; and care was taken to accord no favor to Christianity, or any other supernatural religion, that was denied to Islam. Nationalism became the official Turkish religion. At the same time the army was kept in fighting trim, and nationalist schooling and propaganda were promoted. The Turkish masses were becoming literate and learning from textbooks and over radios that they belonged to a "superior race," being descended (pretty mythically) from highly civilized ancient Hittites, that throughout the ages they

[1] To emphasize the nationalist character of the new Turkey, the Greek name of "Constantinople" was supplanted by the Turkish, "Istanbul."

had had a "mission," and that now they were again fulfilling their destiny as a great race and great nation.

The Persians had a counterpart to Atatürk in Riza Pahlavi, an army officer who forcefully set up a nationalist regime at Teheran and made himself Shah. He introduced into Persia most of the novel laws which were being decreed in Turkey, including those directed against the privileged status of the Muslim religion and aimed at establishing a "modern," secularized, national state, with European dress, calendar, and social usages. Like his Turkish prototype, too, Riza Pahlavi sought to merge the traditional tribalism of his people into a superior national patriotism by teaching them, in army and school and by help of latest technical devices of propaganda, to cherish their distinctive language, their history, and their "mission." In 1934 he announced that the nation would no longer be officially designated by the "corrupt and un-national" name of "Persia," but by the ancient, racial name of "Iran." The Persians, he explained, were the true "Iranians," the pure "Aryans." Which was, so to speak, undercutting the claim of his European contemporary, Adolf Hitler.

The Arabs had been historically both a tribal people and the conquerors and builders of a Muslim empire extending from the Tigris-Euphrates, through Egypt, to the Iberian peninsula. In the late nineteenth and early twentieth centuries, while actually or nominally subject to the Ottoman Empire, they had imbibed from Europe considerable nationalist spirit, particularly in Egypt through British military occupation and control, and in Syria and Iraq through French and American educational institutions and as reaction against "Turkification." This latent nationalism of the Arabs was stimulated and brought to the fore by their common participation during World War I in what "Lawrence of Arabia" and other British agents glowingly described as a war of liberation from the Turks. Freed indeed they were from the Ottoman Empire, but only to be subjected or "mandated" to European powers: Iraq, Jordan, Palestine, Saudi Arabia, and Egypt to Great Britain; Syria and Lebanon to France.

Tribal and separatist traditions were still influential with the Arabs, and, unlike the Turks and the Persians, they had no outstanding and unifying leader. Wherefore in the postwar period their nationalism was exhibited in agitation and insurrection in the several Arab areas against the respective occupying powers, and it did succeed in a gradual lessening of British and French domination. The driving force in this postwar Arab struggle against Western Europe was not religious, as it had been in earlier ages, but nationalistic. In Syria and Lebanon, for instance, the hitherto mutually hostile Christian Arabs and Druse Arabs made common national cause with each other, and with Muslim Arabs, against the French.

On one point all Arabs were firmly united. That was in opposition to the pro-Zionist "Balfour Declaration" and to its postwar implementing by Great Britain, which, as "mandatory," admitted to Palestine a tide of Zionist immigrants that rapidly increased the number of Jews there from barely 70,000 in 1920 to over half a million in 1938. And the number continued to grow, displacing and uprooting an ever larger number of indigenous Arabs. Here, again, it was not a religious conflict between Jews on one hand and Muslims and Christians on the other. It was one nationalism against another. The Zionist Jews were intent on making Palestine theirs; the Arabs, on keeping it theirs. In the circumstances there was incessant incitement to violence. Murders and riots at Jerusalem and in the countryside became chronic. The British government could not satisfy or appease either nationality, and British armed forces maintained only a semblance of order.

The British faced rising native nationalism not only in Palestine and Egypt but also throughout their huge Indian Empire. Here it was sedulously preached by upper- and middle-class intellectuals, organized in an "All-India Congress" party, and most effectively by Mohandas Gandhi, whose ascetic devotion to the masses and idealistic campaign for "nonviolent noncooperation" with the British made him, in native belief, a national saint and earned him the popular title of "Mahatma" ("Great Soul"). In vain the British jailed Gandhi. He simply went on hunger strikes which dramatized to his nationalist following the "martyrdom" he was undergoing at British hands, and yet which the British dared not let culminate in his death lest they be faced not by passive resistance but by active rebellion. In vain certain governmental reforms, including the establishment of some native provincial councils, were enacted by the British at the close of World War I. They were offset by repressive military measures such as the Amritsar "massacre" in which several hundred natives who had assembled to protest against the government were shot down by British troops. In vain the British proposed in 1928 to make more concessions looking toward Indian home rule, and in 1933 still more. Indian nationalists heightened their demands each time, until by 1939 they were demanding full Dominion status on a par with Canada and Australia, or else complete independence.

The Chinese had a tireless apostle of nationalism in Sun Yat-sen, and numerous disciples among others educated in Europe or the United States or at missionary schools in China. And there was strong popular reaction against multiplying foreign aggressions which threatened to subjugate, partition, and subvert the nation. Sun Yat-sen played an inspiring role in the revolution of 1910–1911 which overthrew the imperial regime and instituted the republic, and likewise in the formation of the nationalist party known as the Kuomintang. He was, however, a visionary and propagandist, rather than an organizer, and he failed to unite the country or to repress the anarchy and fighting brought on by rival "war lords." Shortly before his death in 1925 he unwittingly paved the way for later trouble by cooperating with Chinese Communists and accepting aid from the Soviet Union. After his death, nevertheless, he was extolled all over China as a national hero, and his ideas became the inspiration for rapid extension of the Kuomintang.

China, the party declared, must possess a democratic government, a higher standard of living for the masses, and an intensity of national feeling that would preserve its historic territory and distinctive culture and tolerate no foreign interference or tutelage; pending the achievement of these ultimate goals, China must submit to a dictatorship. Such was the nationalist program, and its execution fell to Sun Yat-sen's brother-in-law and military commander, Chiang Kai-shek.

Chiang overcame the war lords, and might possibly have realized in time the dream of a liberal and democratic national state for China if it had not been for Communist hostility and Japanese aggression.

Japan, already emphatically nationalistic before World War I, became more so through its easy conquest and appropriation of German territories in the Far East. Its government fell more and more under the direction of militarists and imperialists, who in 1931–1932 began the conquest of Manchuria and war with China. Thereby was forged a link in the iron chain leading to World War II.

CHAPTER X

Totalitarian Nationalism
and World War II

1. Advent of "Integral" or "Totalitarian" Nationalism

According to Woodrow Wilson, the objective of World War I had been not only to establish a League of Nations for the maintenance of world peace but also "to make the world safe for democracy." That is, political democracy should be coupled with nationalism. And immediately following the war, it seemed as though this ideal was being realized. For outside of Russia, where the Tsarist autocracy was supplanted by a Communist dictatorship, national states both large and small, both new and old, adopted or elaborated democratic forms of government providing for popular elections, parliamentary rule, ministerial responsibility, and personal liberties. In a majority of instances, republican government was preferred over royalist; and women shared, equally with men, the democratic mass suffrage.

Yet the seemingly all-but-universal triumph of political democracy came at the moment when international relations were embittered by the war and by the ensuing peace settlement. It was the moment, too, when the gravest problems of political and economic reconstruction were confronting statesmen and peoples, especially those in defeated and in newly emerging nations. These were apt to be unfamiliar or impatient with the practical operation of political democracy and hence tempted to subvert it with some sort of nationalistic dictatorship.

Of course, nationalism was compatible with democracy. Both

were mass movements, and nationalism was obviously enhanced in countries such as the United States and Great Britain that were experienced in democracy and victorious in war. But nationalism might be even more compatible with dictatorship, particularly if the latter was adept at mass propaganda and acquired mass support. In that case nationalism was more or less sure to be bereft of any liberal feature or international aim which a Woodrow Wilson might attach to it, and to disclose itself as alarmingly "totalitarian" or "integral."

"Integral" is the adjective originally used by Charles Maurras at the height of the "Dreyfus Affair" in France to describe his peculiar brand of nationalism, and that of the *Action française* which he founded. An "integral nationalist," he wrote, "places his country above everything; he therefore conceives, treats, and resolves all questions in their relation to the national interest." Maurras preached a cult of soil and blood, and among things he thought essential to a full reawakening of French nationalism were monarchy, hero worship, and stern repudiation of liberalism and individualism. He denounced "Hebrew Christianity" as a slave religion and Christ's teaching of equality and humility as destructive of needful national egoism; and though himself outside the Catholic Church he paradoxically glorified it for its national role in French history.

This integral nationalism of Maurras bred hatreds. It particularly bred hatred of "alien" influences within France: Jewish, Protestant, Masonic, republican, and, latterly, papal. It likewise campaigned against foreigners: Germans, Englishmen, Americans, and so on. Always it upheld a hundred (or hundred and ten) per cent French nationalism, at once suspicious and forceful; ever expecting the worst and ever preparing against it by urging heavier armaments and more unyielding foreign and colonial policies. There is scarcely conceivable an excess of nationalism beyond the integral variety of Maurras, doctrinaire and demagogue.[1]

[1] For details about Integral Nationalism in France (and Italy), see my *Historical Evolution of Modern Nationalism*, VI, 164–231, and *France, a Nation of Patriots*, 202–205; and also W. C. Buthman, *The Rise of Integral Nationalism in France* (1939).

Yet integral nationalism, foreshadowed by Maurras before World War I, did not obtain deep or lasting lodgment in France. The French people were generally patriotic—even nationalistic—but the nationalism of the large majority remained associated with revolutionary Jacobinism and democratic republicanism. Besides, the French Republic benefited from its war victory and recovery of Alsace-Lorraine, and incidentally from papal condemnation of Maurras and the *Action française*.

It was nations which suffered defeat or grievous disappointment in World War I, most notably Russia, Italy, and Germany, that exemplified integral nationalism, now more usually styled "totalitarian." To be sure, the dictatorship which Lenin and his successors exercised in Russia was Communist (and professedly internationalist), rather than nationalist, but in reality, as we have indicated in an earlier chapter,[1] it aroused and exploited popular patriotism for its totalitarian ends. It was the stimulation of nationalist sentiment among the Russian masses, as well as the organizing ability of Leon Trotsky, that frustrated foreign attempts, first of Germany and then of the Allies, to oust the Bolsheviks in 1918–1920. In turn the Bolsheviks tightened their hold upon the masses by fusing nationalist with Communist policies and propaganda in an essentially police state. Russia's economic isolation, the cutting off of trade and travel with the rest of Europe, the inculcation of a suspicious if not belligerent attitude toward other nations, the rigid compulsory disciplining of the masses by means of national army, national schools, and secret police, the fostering of a cult of Russian music and ballet, Russian art, Russian science and technology, of such historic Russian "heroes" as Ivan the Terrible and Peter the Great, and above all, of the Communist Trinity—Marx, Lenin, and Stalin—all this made for nationalism that was fanatical and totalitarian. And the Communist dictatorship, imbued with Marxian materialism, naturally sought to exterminate Christianity and any other supernatural religion, and to substitute for it a this-worldly atheism. Atheism, however, has been too rarefied, too negative, except for an elite. For the masses the

[1] See ch. II, pp. 16–18, above.

religion of nationalism is sufficiently this-worldly and much more moving.

Italy at the close of World War I seemed committed, in common with other nations of central and western Europe, to liberal democracy. In fact, however, it was more sorely beset with postwar difficulties than any of the other Allies (except Russia). Economic conditions were bad. National pride was piqued by the curbing of imperial ambitions in Africa and across the Adriatic. Supporters of the parliamentary regime were split into rival parties and factions, with no outstanding leader or statesman. In the circumstances two different trends toward dictatorship appeared. One was Socialist, from the extreme Left, inspired by Russian communism. The other was Nationalist, from the extreme Right, put in motion by D'Annunzio's fevered speeches and dramatic seizure of Fiume. How akin were the two extremes was revealed by the tactics of revolutionary mob violence which both employed, and, in a personal way, by the totalitarian dictator, the *Duce*, who presently stepped on the Italian stage—and on the Italian people.

Benito Mussolini had been identified during most of his life with left-wing Marxian socialism, serving it in exile and in journalism, and, like the majority of the "comrades," being very critical of Italy's imperialistic war of 1911–1912 with Turkey. He did perform the prescribed military service for his country, and, unlike many Italian Socialists, he defended participation in World War I on grounds that Italy as a "proletarian" nation was obligated by the doctrine of class conflict to war against the "capitalist" empire of Austria-Hungary, and that the surest means of converting the Italian masses to socialism was to associate it with a national cause. He seems to have momentarily hesitated at the end of the war whether to continue Leftist or to seek fame and fortune on the Nationalist Right. He chose the latter course: it bade fair to be more popular and to serve better his ego.

So Mussolini's Fascist movement came into being. It borrowed Communist methods, while indulging in counterviolence against the "Reds"; and so popular was its appeal, and so rapid its growth, that by 1924 it was in power. The nationalism it represented was truly totalitarian. Mussolini, *Duce* and dictator, posed as Caesar and rivaled Mark Antony in grandiloquence. Italians were ceaselessly reminded of their past greatness and future destiny as a nation. Economic nationalism was intensified. National schooling was promoted, and national press censorship and national police control were of course imposed. National armaments were built up. National imperialism was forwarded. Fascist shirts and salutes and parades betokened a nationalist religion, though this was somewhat less intolerant than its counterpart in Communist Russia. In Italy there was too much popular respect for the papacy and devotion to Catholic Christianity to allow of open or speedy break between totalitarian state and historic church. In fact Mussolini, hoping to gain Catholic support, consented, by the Lateran Treaty of 1929, to a concordat with the Church and the creation within Rome of the tiny but sovereign papal state of the Vatican. Friction persisted, nevertheless. Catholicism and Fascism were fundamentally incompatible. Strictures on Catholic activities by the Fascist dictatorship, and its promulgation of anti-Semitic decrees, evoked vigorous protests from the Pope.

The perfect exemplar of integral, totalitarian nationalism was not Mussolini (or Stalin). It was Adolf Hitler. Mussolini possessed a sense of humor and was something of an opportunist, but not so the solemn and fanatical Hitler. Hitler had been born in Austria of a family of the lower middle class and had grown up with only ordinary schooling and frustrated ambition. As a youth he had failed to gain admission to the Academy of Painting at Vienna and then had eked out a meager livelihood as a freelance illustrator at Munich, solacing himself meanwhile with enthusiastic appreciation of Wagner's operas, Nietzsche's philosophy of the superman, and the anti-Semitic writings of Adolf Stöcker and Stewart Chamberlain. He was already an ardent German nationalist when World War I began. Though still an Austrian citizen, he enlisted in the German army, and in it he served throughout the war. He was awarded an iron cross for valor, but was never promoted beyond the rank of corporal; and his cup of bitterness was filled to overflowing when the victory of the Allies was followed by Republican revolution within Germany. "My brow burned with shame," he wrote, "and my hatred against the men who had brought about this crime grew and grew; I decided to become a politician."

Shortly after the war, therefore, Hitler joined with a handful of his youthful army acquaintances in forming the National Socialist (or Nazi) party. The party's program denounced the Paris peace settlement and demanded the union of all Germans in a Greater Germany, the return of the German colonies, and the unrestricted rearming of Germany. It assailed Jews within Germany as "aliens," denied them German citizenship, and threatened them with exile or extinction. It proposed to prohibit foreign immigration, to ban all "unpatriotic" newspapers and organizations, to nationalize popular education, and to enact economic reforms in harmony with the principle of national, rather than Marxian, socialism. It condemned the "corrupting parliamentary system" and championed professional representation directed by "a strong central authority," which meant a nationalist dictatorship. Almost simultaneously with the issuance of this program, Hitler joyfully discovered that he had oratorical ability and a gift of showmanship, that by "letting himself go," amid dramatic stage settings, in frenzied exposition of woes and wrongs of Germany and in fierce cursing of Jews and foreigners, he could attract and hold large audiences. To a person who had been thwarted all his life, it was very gratifying to know that he had at least one talent which he could put to effective use. His ego swelled.

Hitler did not immediately realize his vaulting ambition. The Republican coalition of right-wing Socialists, Catholics, and Democrats managed for ten years to carry general elections and keep a parliamentary majority. But it was difficult to reconcile differences within the coalition, and to safeguard it against growth of a pro-Russian Communist party on one side and an even more ominous growth of the Nazi party on the other. Especially the latter resorted to violence and the recruiting of private armed forces, and it profited from broadening popular reaction against the territorial losses, the military restrictions, and the financial burdens imposed on Germany by the Allies. The economic depression of 1929–1930 was the last straw, so to speak, which broke the back of the democratic Republic. By 1933 the Nazis were in power, with Hitler as Chancellor and dictator. The next year he assumed the honorific supreme title of *Reichsführer*, and Germans were saluting him with raised fist and loud *Heil!*

We need not here recount the story of Hitler's totalitarian Germany from 1933 to 1939.[1] We all know that Jews (including Christians with Jewish blood) were outrageously persecuted, that Marxians and Liberals were alike silenced, that arbitrary arrests and bloody "purges" were carried out, that youth was rigidly indoctrinated in school and university; that the country's great industrial wealth and resources were concentrated on armaments, and that the considerable opposition of Christians, both Protestant and Catholic, was forcefully repressed. Above all, nationalism was made the alpha and omega—the veritable religion—of the state.

Establishment of dictatorships in Germany, Italy, and Russia affected and was imitated in other European countries that had seemed immediately after the war to be committed to democracy. Some, in fear of Communist Russia or Nazi Germany, succumbed to military dictatorship: Hungary, Poland, Lithuania, Latvia, Estonia, Austria. Others, troubled by domestic factionalism and turbulence, yielded to royal or reactionary dictatorships: Portugal, Spain, Yugoslavia, Rumania, Bulgaria, Greece. We have elsewhere mentioned the special revolutionary dictatorships of Mustafa Kemal in Turkey and Riza Pahlavi in Iran.[2] All such dictatorships, however variant in motivation or conduct, were emphatically nationalist.

2. Features of the New Totalitarian Dictatorship

Some general reflections may here be offered about the totalitarian and dictatorial type of nationalism which arose in Russia, Italy, and

---

[1] Its essence can best be understood by reading Hitler's *Mein Kampf*, the "bible" of the Nazis, an excellent English translation of which was published in 1941 under the editorship of George N. Shuster.

[2] See above, pp. 131–132.

Germany after World War I and which was destined to lead to World War II.[1] First, while dictatorship itself was no novelty in the long history of European civilization, a new genus of dictator now appeared. Previously the successful despot normally came of good family and possessed better-than-average education and considerable military fame. That was the case alike with Greek tyrants of antiquity and with Latin-American dictators of the last century. Alexander the Great had been tutored by no less a scholar than Aristotle; Caesar was a distinguished historian as well as general and dictator; and it would be hard to find any petty South American dictator who had not commanded at least a regiment and fortified himself with the positivist philosophy of Auguste Comte. Certainly the Italian despots of early modern times were men of both culture and prowess, and the royal despots of the eighteenth century were products of selective eugenics and meticulous education. Even Napoleon was a scion of the Corsican aristocracy and a graduate of the aristocratic French military school of Brienne; he was the foremost general, before becoming the most feared dictator, of his age.

In contrast with the quality and training of earlier dictators, note who and what the newer ones are. There is Hitler, who, as we have already suggested, was quite plebeian, with neither intellectual nor military distinction. There is Mussolini, whose father was a blacksmith, whose formal education was acquired in a minor normal school, whose career was that of an unsuccessful elementary school teacher and a second-rate journalist, and whose military service was brief and inconspicuous. There is Stalin, generated by a peasant shoemaker, dismissed from a church seminary at the age of seventeen for misbehavior and lack of discipline, self-trained in the strong-arm arts of highway robbery and factory disorder, and, as a convicted criminal, relieved of any military service in World War I. These newer dictators came from the masses, and theirs was a national mass dictatorship.

[1] These reflections were set forth originally, in greater detail, in "The Novelty of Totalitarianism in the History of Western Civilization," *Proceedings of the American Philosophical Society*, LXXXII (1940).

Secondly, the newer dictatorship was really totalitarian. It monopolized all powers and directed all national activities. It subordinated to itself all economic, religious, educational, and cultural institutions and policies. It left no room for the free play of individual wills and recognized no utility in free inquiry. On the contrary, it sought to make everyone conform to the will and thought of the governing party and dictator. Alike to Communists, Fascists, and Nazis, the totalitarian national state was omniscient and infallible as well as omnipotent. In all these respects the Russia of Stalin was far more nationally intolerant than the Russia of the Tsars had been; the Germany of Hitler, than divine-right monarchy of Hohenzollern or Habsburg.

Thirdly, and particularly important, the newer despotism commanded and relied upon patriotic mass support. It was no affair of an aristocratic class or military caste. It was frankly for and by sufferance of the half-educated and half-propertied lower middle class and upper proletariat and an ever enlarging bureaucracy. It sprang from and returned to the great median of what were truly the masses, and everyone above or below who was not sychophantic was suspect and liable to liquidation. Previous European regimes may have been aristocratic or plutocratic, but they had normally showed a tolerance for the masses which these, under the new dictatorship, seldom evinced for the classes.

Fourthly, totalitarian and dictatorial nationalism was maintained, and mass support of it assured, by novel and marvelously effective agencies of popular education and propaganda. Radio and amplifier had come only in the wake of World War I; the cinema, only on its eve. The production of cheap wood-pulp paper, with resulting large-scale journalism, had begun only in the 1890's; compulsory school attendance only in the 1880's and then in only a very few countries. Now all these agencies were perfected, and ready to be seized upon and used by a nationalist dictator. Not alone in Hitlerian Germany but more sensationally in Russia under Stalin and in Italy under Mussolini, children were put in state schools and forcibly fed with mental pabulum nicely calculated to make them unquestioning devotees of a given brand of national ideology. Everyone was taught to read, of course; that was a favorite boast of the newer dictators. It flattered the masses, and probably rendered them more gullible than they would have been if they had remained illiterate. For what they now read, and heard, was as closely prescribed or censored as the content of their schooling. The whole publishing business was "coordinated" (that is the technical term); and there was nothing to read of which the national state disapproved. Cinema and radio were outright state monopolies; the one flicked at the popular eye, the other dinned into the popular ear, only what the regime adjudged advantageous to itself; and Hitler with an amplifier was more frightening than Napoleon had been without one.

It is to be noted, moreover, that while all three of the outstanding dictators of the era were skeptical about Christianity, contemptuous of its moral teachings, and bent on subjugating if not destroying it, they patronized and inculcated in their following an emotional and essentially religious devotion. Especially Communist Russia and Nazi Germany were "churches" as well as states, each with its dictator as *pontifex maximus;* and they were churches not old and staid and conventional, but pristine and zealous. Their creeds (that is, their ideologies) were novel; their banners and rituals and slogans were novel—and attractive. No wonder that their converts were numerous, particularly among the young. Persons who had lost or were deprived of contact with the Christian or Jewish God, wanted new gods, and now they got them: in Germany, a Dionysus-like tribal god of blood and soil; in Russia, a Lucretian god of fatalism and materialism; both attended by plenty of ritual, sermons, and fanaticism.

Furthermore, the new type of totalitarian dictatorship evolved a new pattern of political methods and techniques. Behind a mask of plebiscites, popular elections, and occasional assemblings of a so-called parliament—which could listen and applaud, but not really parley—the government actually functioned through and with a single political party which comprised a minority, usually a small minority, of the nation, and which was more or less hand-picked, severely disciplined, and on occasion "purged," and which had a monopoly of the means of influencing public opinion and enforcing the will of the dictator. The party, under the dictator, permeated and ultimately dominated the army, the courts, the ubiquitous secret police, the schools and universities, the newspapers, radios and cinemas, the telegraphs and telephones, the pulpits and rostrums, the arts and amusements, the youth organizations, indeed all organizations whether economic, social, or cultural. A Russian Tsar, a Louis XIV, or an Alexander the Great, might well envy the speed and effectiveness with which dissenters and doubters were liquidated and suspects gathered into concentration camps.

Still another, and a most significant, novelty of totalitarian nationalist dictatorship was its exalting of might and force, not only as means to an end—there had been many precedents for that—but as an end in itself. In earlier and less totalitarian days, a despot who got rid of a foe or appropriated some neighbor's land went to considerable trouble, as a rule, to justify his action on conventional moral grounds. Now, the dictator was hardly expected to offer any explanation at all, and if he did it bore no trace of the Decalogue or the Sermon on the Mount. It sufficed to echo the more up-to-date Nietzschean and pseudo-Darwinian principles that patience is a vice and that progress depends on a struggle for existence and *Lebensraum* for the fittest. Or it might suffice to recite the Marxian creed that proletarians have to fight and they are always right. The fact remained that brute force was the determinant in the internal affairs and foreign policies of the totalitarian national state. It was the forcefulness of these states, and the lack of it in the democratic states of the West, which brought on World War II.

3. *Aggressions of Nationalist Dictators*

The totalitarian dictatorships flourished, we have said, in nations which felt aggrieved by defeat in World War I, or, as in the case of Italy, by failure to obtain expected advantages from the peace settlement. Suffering from a kind of inferiority-superiority complex, they sought compensation through aggression, or the threat of aggression, against their neighbors and former foes. To get what they wanted (and they wanted a lot) they would back up diplomacy with preparedness for war. On the other hand, the Western democracies made it easier for the dictatorships to pursue aggressive policies by reason of their own reputed victory in World War I and comparative satisfaction with the peace. They showed themselves smug, self-centered, jealous of one another, and, what was especially ominous, pacific to the extent of reducing their armaments and meeting the dictators' increase with "appeasement." The United States went so far in nationalist isolation as to pledge itself to neutrality in future wars. And naturally in the circumstances the League of Nations proved an extremely weak reed for propping up world peace.

The powder-train of bellicose aggressions which eventually exploded in World War II, started with Japan's seizure of Manchuria from China in 1931–1934. Japan had previously made heavy but futile demands on Chiang Kai-shek and his Nationalist China. Now Japan, yielding to an ultrapatriotic military clique and accepting a practically totalitarian dictatorship, pressed its imperialistic demands with renewed energy and determination. China appealed to the League of Nations for help. The League's response was the appointment of a special committee which, after six months' investigation, recommended the censuring of Japan. Japan calmly ignored the recommendation and withdrew from the League. The League, unable or unwilling to adopt any "sanctions," merely expressed "regret." Nor was China's appeal to the United States more successful. It was left to bear alone the crushing weight of Japanese arms.

After occupying Manchuria, Japan opened full-scale war with China, conquering Peking and the coastal areas, setting up a puppet regime at Nanking, and forcing Chiang Kai-shek to fall back to the remote city of Chungking. Imperial nationalist ambition of the Japanese military soared ever higher. They talked about creating, under their guidance, a "co-prosperity sphere" which would include the whole of China and quite possibly, in addition, the Philippines, Indo-China, Indonesia, Malaya, and Burma, perhaps even India.

Hitler and Mussolini did not need the example of Japan's aggression in Manchuria to commit aggressions of their own, though they were doubtless heartened by its success. Mussolini overpowered Ethiopia with Italian armies and annexed it, defying and withdrawing from the League of Nations when it protested and France and Britain half-heartedly agreed to impose economic "sanctions." He sent troops to aid General Franco in the Spanish Civil War, probably in the hope of being recompensed by cession of all or part of the Balearic Islands. He seized and subjugated the kingdom of Albania across the Adriatic. He let loose a flood of nationalist propaganda against Great Britain for its critical attitude toward his activities in Africa and Spain, and especially against France for its retention of what he claimed were rightful Italian possessions: Savoy and Nice and Tunis.

Hitler and his Nazis were even bolder, even more unscrupulous in violating pledges and tearing up treaties; and this went on with impunity for six years. In clear violation of the Paris peace settlement, Germany was fully and superbly rearmed. Its air force was given a tryout, along with Italian troops, in the Spanish Civil War. And further fortified by alliance with Fascist Italy—the so-called Axis—and by friendly understanding with militarist Japan, Nazi Germany invaded and annexed Austria. Then, with Britain and France still appeasing, and the United States still indifferent and aloof, it subjugated first a part, and soon the whole, of Czechoslovakia. Only when it threatened Poland with like partition (and likely extinction) did the two democratic great powers of western Europe take a positive stand against totalitarian aggression and agree to use force, if necessary, to protect Poland. Unfortunately, their force was not equal to Nazi Germany's and they failed to enlist the support of Communist Russia whose Dictator, Stalin, and his foreign minister, Molotov, perceived greater opportunities for aggressive expansion of the Soviet Union in alliance with Hitler than in opposition to him.

4. World War II

On August 23, 1939, a virtual alliance was signed at Moscow between Communist Russia and Nazi Germany. On September 1, Germany launched a slashing attack upon Poland with massed infantry spearheaded by armored tanks and intensive air bombardment. Two days later, Britain and France declared war on Germany. It was the start of World War II.

We need not here recount in any detail the story of the war. The previous World War had lasted four years; this one, six years, and it was fought with all the deadly weapons of the earlier one, and such new instruments as guided missiles and the culminating atomic bombs; and it was fraught with wider and worse destruction. We may simply recall that Poland was quickly knocked out and partitioned between Germany and the Soviet Union, that then German troops occupied neutral Norway, Denmark, the Netherlands, Belgium, and Luxembourg, expelled a British expeditionary force from the Continent, and swept over France, bringing about its capitulation. Within a year, complete and final victory appeared to be in the grasp of Nazi Germany. It had ended all armed resistance on the Continent. Its Axis partner, Fascist Italy, had actively joined it. Communist Russia had been bought off and was adhering to a benevolent neutrality. Friendly Japan was amply proving its preeminent prowess in the Far East.

Only Great Britain was yet to be overborne. Indeed it might well have been, except for the inspiriting leadership of its redoubtable Winston Churchill, the stubborn patriotic endurance of its people, the doughtiness of its airmen, the military supplies furnished it by the United States and Canada, and the mad blunderings of the Nazi and Fascist dictators. At the critical moment, instead of concentrating efforts and resources on the task of invading and occupying Britain, Hitler broke with Stalin and directed massive invasion of Russia, while Mussolini made calamitous attempts to seize Egypt and Greece.

As for the United States, it gradually, under the astute guidance of Franklin Roosevelt, came step by step out of its isolation. Its community of language with England and its liberal democratic traditions naturally rendered it sympathetic with Great Britain and inimical toward Nazi Germany, and the majority of its people felt growing alarm about threats to American security from the Axis in the Atlantic and from Japan in the Pacific. The United States accordingly, and in increasing violation of neutrality, provided the British with strategic war supplies and withheld them from the Japanese. The upshot, we know, was the Japanese attack at Pearl Harbor, followed quickly by American declaration of war against Japan, and declarations of war by Japan's allies, Germany and Italy, against the United States.

Once the United States was actually at war, it applied itself wholeheartedly, with nationalist fervor, to winning the war. So, too, did the Soviet Union under Stalin. Both countries suffered grave initial setbacks, the one from Japanese military and naval victories in the Philippines and adjacent Pacific; the other from deep and terrifying German invasion. Eventually, however, the war-making potentialities of the United States and the Soviet Union, and the unwavering national patriotism of their respective peoples, together with Britain's strength and dogged perserverance, outweighed everything the opposing dictators of the Axis and Japan could command. "Undergrounds" of nationalist disaffection spread in Axis-conquered countries, and revolt simmered within Italy and Germany. At the last, in Europe, as Anglo-American forces overran Italy and those of the United States, Britain, and Canada, with "Free French," made juncture with Russian armies in mid-Germany, Mussolini was caught fleeing toward Switzerland and summarily put to death, and Hitler, a maniacal refugee in a Berlin dugout, committed suicide and his body was burned. Slightly over three months later, American dropping of atom bombs on Hiroshima and Nagasaki ended Japan's belligerence and brought surrender or suicide of its war lords.

CHAPTER XI

Contemporary World-Wide Nationalism

1. Nationalist Imperialism of Communist Russia

World War II was even more of a nationalist struggle than World War I had been. It was waged from start to finish by national states whose peoples stuck to fighting unless and until they met military disaster and overwhelming defeat. True, the dictatorial, totalitarian type of nationalism, as represented by German Nazis and Italian Fascists, was discredited and done away with, but the succeeding democratic republicanism in Italy and West Germany did not lack nationalist spirit and import. Moreover, the United States was now foremost in resuscitating and supporting a league of nations, re-christened "United Nations," as a federation of national states charged with the preservation of international peace. Within a dozen years, this world organization, with its seat in New York, had eighty-two members, comprising twenty-six national states in Europe, twenty-three in Asia, twenty-two in the Americas, nine in Africa, and two in the South Pacific. The whole world, and not merely Europe, was thus being put on a nationality basis.

Actually, nevertheless, it proved extremely difficult to establish or maintain peace after World War II. For several years Communist nationalist Russia, flushed with its hard-fought success in the war, and keeping its armed forces at war strength, pursued aggressive policies in both Europe and Asia unhampered by military opposition of other prewar great powers. Germany, Japan, and Italy were now disarmed and garrisoned by foreign troops. Great Britain and France were exhausted, and beset by grave domestic problems. The United States, potentially strong, went back to a peace footing, optimistically imagining that Russia would do likewise, and trusting, perhaps too much, in the United Nations.

In the power vacuum thus created, the Soviet dictatorship was free to act. It blocked the holding of any general peace congress; and wherever Russian troops were occupying the whole or part of a country at the end of the fighting, there they lingered, enabling the Communist dictatorship to install satellite regimes. Gradually, we know, the United States discovered that its ideal of democratic liberal nationalism was being threatened and thwarted by dictatorship of the Communist variety quite as much as it had been by Fascist or Nazi. So it belatedly undertook to curb further Russian conquest and subjugation. It rearmed. It formed defensive alliances with other free nations (NATO, SEATO, and others) and stiffened their resistance to communism by granting them economic and military assistance. It surrounded the Soviet Empire with a string of naval and air bases.

Thus on the heels of World War II ensued a "cold war," with the United States and the Soviet Union as leading adversaries, both backed by patriotic mass support at home, and both using the United Nations as sounding board for rival accusations and propaganda. Only after much haggling were peace treaties concluded with Italy and Japan, and also with Austria, which was detached anew from Germany and "neutralized." Yet fifteen years after World War II, Germany itself was still occupied by foreign troops; Russia and the United States (and their respective satellites and allies) could reach no agreement on peace terms.

Meanwhile, before it was halted by American and West European opposition, the Soviet Union had mightily expanded into a vast Communist Empire. Not only did it annex outright the lands and peoples it had appropriated while in alliance with Nazi Germany (the eastern half of Poland and the whole of Lithuania, Latvia, and Estonia, together with strips of Rumania and Finland), but it now turned into dependencies most of the remaining national states of eastern and east-central Europe (Poland, Rumania, Yugoslavia, Albania, Bulgaria, Hungary, and Czechoslovakia). It also dominated, while partitioning, the eastern half of Germany: a part it nominally ceded to dependent Communist Poland as "compensation" for its seizure of Poland's eastern provinces; another and smaller part it annexed outright; and the remainder it made into a German Communist satellite. Besides, by going to war with Japan at the last moment of World War II, Russia was enabled to regain the northern pacific islands it had lost in the Russo-Japanese War of 1904–1905, and also to be of decisive help to Chinese Communists in expelling Chiang Kai-shek from the mainland and establishing allied Communist regimes in China and in northern Korea and northern Vietnam.

Here, clearly, was imperialism, but an imperialism with a difference from that which had characterized the prewar era. This was a strictly "Eastern" Communist imperialism, and it was conducted in the name, and ostensibly in the interest, of indigenous nationalism. Like Ukrainians, Byelorussians, and other peoples within the original Soviet Union, the newly subjected peoples—Poles, Rumanians, Germans, Hungarians, Koreans, and all the others—were permitted the form of national states and the possession of such features of cultural nationalism as native language and literature and certain historic traditions. In other words, Soviet imperialism was not exclusively an expression of Russian nationalism, but an attractive recognition of the nationalism of other peoples. It especially appealed to "backward" peoples, particularly to those in Asia and Africa that had been dominated by the imperialist powers of Western Europe. Throughout Latin America, likewise, Communist infiltration grew and exercised increasing influence by masquerading as a popular nationalist movement and campaigning zealously against "Yankee imperialism and exploitation." This was the burden, for example, of Fidel Castro's revolutionary regime in Cuba and its flirtation with the Soviet Union.

Apparently "Holy Russia" has a special appeal to predominantly agricultural peoples of the world which "Happy America" lacks. The very opposition of a great industrial nation like the United States seems to commend Communist nationalism to such peoples, all the more because the Russians, like them, were not so long ago a peasant nation.

2. Native Nationalism Versus Western Imperialism

In fact, a most significant outcome of World War II, and a ubiquitous feature of the present age is the *world-wide* ebullience of nationalism. Nationalism is no longer a preeminently European (and American) phenomenon. From imported seed, it is now in flower in every clime and on every continent.

As indicated in the preceding chapter, nationalism was becoming a major force in Asia and in parts of Africa before World War II. It was then being absorbed by native leaders through schooling in Europe or other contact with Europeans, and by them it was being agitated among the masses. Nationalist political parties were already very active in India and China, in Turkey and Iran, in Egypt and other Arab lands.

World War II was the decisive factor in the world-wide triumph of nationalism and the accompanying repudiation and overthrow of Western imperialism. This was more truly a world war than World War I had been, and its effects were correspondingly more far-reaching. It was waged all over the Far East, across the breadth of North Africa, and in strategic spots of the Near East; and the natives in these areas witnessed at close range the repeated military setbacks to Western imperial powers. Arabs were fully aware of French impotence in Syria and North Africa, and of British reverses in Egypt and Greece. Peoples of the Far and Middle East were deeply impressed by the ease with which non-European Japan ousted the French from Indo-China, the British from Burma and Malaya, the Dutch from Indonesia, and the Americans from the Philippines, and installed native governments with the slogan "Asia for the Asians." Eventually, as we know, Japan was defeated and, along with Italy, obliged to surrender its colonies and conquests, just as Germany had been forced to surrender hers after World War I. But, this time, other imperial powers of Western Europe did not profit as they had previously done. They had now lost too much prestige, and were far too weakened by World War II, to cope successfully with the persistent and militant demand of colonial peoples for national independence.

Such demand was abetted and utilized, as we have just remarked, by the Soviet Union in order to combat its Western rivals in the "cold war" and to win converts to communism among the teeming millions of Asia and Africa (and Latin America). Russian propaganda, as well as Russian arms, contributed immensely to the Communist victory in China, North Korea, and North Vietnam. To be sure, the ceaseless tirades of the Soviet Union against Western imperialism might be masking an Eastern imperialism of its own—and so, too, those of Communist China. But that seemed to matter little to peoples devoted to assailing and getting rid of the Western imperialism with which they were familiar.

The United States, also, now championed native rights and native rule. Its prewar promise of independence to the Philippines was honored in 1946; in 1952 Puerto Rico was made a self-governing "commonwealth"; in 1959 Hawaii was admitted to the Union as a sovereign state. American sympathy with the national aspirations of all kinds of colonial peoples, and American economic aid to them, were both heightened by rivalry with the Communist Empire and a desire to counteract its influence.

Unable to breast the postwar tidal wave of nationalism, Great Britain more or less gracefully, and with only occasional delaying action, parted with the bulk of its overseas possessions. Its vast Indian Empire was broken up and partitioned among four independent national states: India proper, Pakistan, Burma, and Ceylon. Palestine passed mainly to the new national Zionist state of Israel; and, step by step, control of Egypt (with the Suez Canal) and other Arab states, and also of Græco-Turkish Cyprus, was surrendered. Full independence was accorded not only to the Irish Republic (Eire), but also to Malaya and Singapore in southeast Asia, and in Africa to the Anglo-Egyptian Sudan, to Ghana, and to Nigeria.

And to all other British possessions in Africa, as in the British West Indies, some sort of national self-government, if not outright independence, has been granted or promised. Certain of the newly freed states belong to the British Commonwealth, but this is a merely nominal bond of union, a formal alliance of sovereign nations.

The Dutch Netherlands was slower in acceding to nationalist demands from its East Indian empire. Nevertheless, it lacked the means of enforcing its rule and putting down rebellion; and its offers of qualified autonomy were rejected. At last it has been constrained to recognize a fully independent Indonesia and to quit all the islands except still disputed New Guinea.

The postwar story of imperial France is similiar. It had to abandon Syria and Lebanon while the war was still in progress; and afterwards its attempt to retain a hold on the rest of its overseas possessions and peoples by associating them with itself in a "French Union," proved a failure. Nor did success attend its subsequent use of force. Both Tunis and Morocco won independence. Protracted fighting in Indo-China ended in French defeat and withdrawal, and an unstable partition of the territory among free native states of Cambodia, Laos, and South Vietnam, and a satellite of Communist China (North Vietnam). Even more protracted and costly has been the insurrection of indigenous Muslim nationalists in Algeria, which has been vehemently opposed by the fairly large minority of French immigrants, but which French armies have failed to overcome; it seems likely that the outcome, sooner or later, will be Algerian independence. Already, the nationalist Fifth French Republic of General De Gaulle has assured the right of national self-determination to the several provinces of the vast tropical territories of French West Africa and French Equatorial Africa. One of these provinces—French Guinea—promptly voted to separate from France and to unite with independent Ghana. The other seven, together with Madagascar, have become independent republics, loosely and temporarily allied with France in a "French Community."

We may here round out our summary by remarking that Libya is now independent, and so, too, is Somalia (a union of former Italian and British colonies); that Belgium has yielded to demands of native tribesmen for freedom of the Congo; that nationalist unrest is simultaneously stirring in the old Portuguese African empire.

Nor does the special kind of Russian Communist imperialism seem impervious to abrasive nationalism. At any rate, a superior nationalist loyalty has alienated Communist Yugoslavia from the Soviet Union and most probably would do the same in Hungary, Poland, Czechoslovakia, and East Germany were it not for repression, or the threat of repression, by Russian armed intervention. And Communist China, with its own nationalism and imperial ambitions, is not likely, in the long run, to take orders from Moscow.

3. *Ambiguous Character of Nationalism in Asia and Africa*

It must be emphasized that the nationalism so conspicuous today in Asia and Africa derives from Europe and yet differs from its source in important respects. While it represents an emotional reaction and hostility of "colonial" peoples to Western imperialism, it aims, of course, as did its European prototype, at replacing alien sway or tutelage with native sovereign states. Yet unlike older European national states, the newer, nationalistically inspired ones outside Europe (and America) are based less frequently at present on linguistic nationality than on racial or religio-cultural peculiarities. For example, a common "nationalist" impulse throughout the huge and heterogeneous British Empire of India has issued in the emergence of separate nations not of distinctive language, but rather of distinctive religion: Hindu India, Muslim Pakistan, Buddhist Burma, and "primitively" Buddhist Ceylon. Throughout most of Africa, nationalism has a racial complexion: in the Union of South Africa, that of white Boers against native blacks; elsewhere, that of blacks or browns against immigrant whites.

In Europe and America, common and distinctive language has been a most important mark and guarantor of nationality, and a fundamental unifying feature of the national state. The only seeming exceptions are trilingual Switzerland and bilingual Canada and Belgium. We should bear in mind, however, that the first two are federal states with a common language for each canton or province, that the third treats French and Flemish as equally official, and that in all three states what may properly be called "subnationalisms" conform with linguistic divisions. The importance of a single language for a national state has been magnified, of course, by the exigencies of popular schooling, with attendant popular literacy and popular journalism.

So long as the masses of a country are largely illiterate, as is the present case in emergent independent states in Asia and Africa, it matters relatively little whether the vernaculars are few or many. To be sure, the national leaders in such states must have, for propagandist purposes, command of the chief spoken languages, and, to intensify popular nationalism and build truly national states after the European model, they will naturally promote popular schooling and literacy. And this requires the use of some particular language, one that can be transformed from a spoken vernacular into a literary *national* language.

To make boundaries of language coincide with those of states has been a gradual and difficult achievement in Europe. It promises to be more protracted and much more difficult in Asia and especially in Africa. India, for instance, harbors three different linguistic "families": (1) Indo-European, with nineteen languages, including Hindi, Bengali, Bihari, Marathi, and Urdu; (2) Dravidian, with fourteen languages, including Tamil and Telegu; and (3) Munda, with ten different dialects. In 1958, following much disputing and rioting among the linguistic groups, the country's political map was redrawn so that a majority of the population of each of fourteen federated provinces (or "states"), except Bombay and Punjab, would speak one and the same vernacular or closely related dialects. Rioting still continued in the state of Bombay between two linguistic entities, the one of thirty million speaking Marathi and the other of nineteen million speaking Gujerati, with the result that, eventually in 1960, Bombay has been split into the two "states" of Maharashtra and Gujerat. In Punjab demands for separate statehood grow louder among the religiously distinctive Sikhs.

Independent India is thus, strictly speaking, not a national state, but either an empire or a federation of national states. What helps to hold it together, and for the present to maintain a kind of domestic internationalism, is the fact that most educated persons throughout the country know and can use a common language—the English language—which, ironically enough, they have acquired from that Western imperialism they so diligently condemn.

India's central government, under Nehru's leadership, has aspired, as would any up-to-date nationalist regime, to create a literate nation through mass schooling in a common native language. Wherefore, at the outset of Indian independence in 1950, it was enacted that Hindi, a major tongue of the North, should be the whole country's "official" language and that the official use of English should be temporary and should terminate in 1965. Obviously, as the Indian masses— over four hundred million of them—become schooled and literate, it is not likely to be in English. Nor is it likely to be in a single local language like Hindi, but rather in a variety of familiar vernaculars. In which case India could hardly be a unitary national state, but at best a federation of diverse language groups consisting, not simply of two or three as in Canada or Switzerland, but, vastly more complex, of fifteen or twenty.

It has been one thing for India, in the pursuit of nationalism, to cast off imperial British rule; it is quite another to prevent, in the long run, India's disintegration into a congeries of rival and quarrelsome linguistic nationalities and national states.

What is true of India in this respect is true, in only lesser degree, of Pakistan. This country consists of two geographically and linguistically separate parts: West Pakistan, with Urdu as the predominant language, and East Pakistan, with Bengali; the two have in common only the Muslim religion and an historic hostility to Hinduism.

In Burma, a majority of the population speak Burmese, though large minorities use Karen or some dialect of Thai. In Ceylon are two unrelated native languages: Indo-Iranian Sinhalese, and Dravidian Tamil. In Malaya are four "official" languages: Malay, Tamil, Mandarin Chinese, and English. In Indonesia are Malay and Dyak, each with differing dialects, and, here and there, Chinese and even, among intellectuals, Dutch!

It is notable, in this connection, that one small new Asian state— that of Israel—has succeeded in artificially establishing and disseminating among its people a common national language. As its nationalist leader, David Ben-Gurion, says: "Only a hundred years ago there was not a single Jew in the world whose mother tongue was Hebrew; today it is the spoken language of hundreds of thousands."[1]

4. Nationalism and Tribalism in Africa

In Africa, very few of the so-called "national states" which are now gaining independence or autonomy, correspond with any ethnic or linguistic unit. In the main they retain the arbitrary colonial boundaries previously fixed for them by European imperial powers, and each includes a medley of *tribes* which have survived from prehistoric times and which severally possess peculiar customs and speech.

No one knows the precise number of tribes on the continent, but nearly a thousand languages are spoken, and there must be at least as many tribes as languages. The late Sir Harry Johnston, famous administrator and linguist, listed 276 Bantu languages alone. Christian missionaries have translated the New Testament into 82 major tongues. In the newly independent state of Ghana, with less than five million inhabitants, over twenty vernaculars are spoken and the government radio broadcasts in six African languages. Ghana is not unique in this regard. South of the Sahara, divers tribal languages or dialects are characteristic of all of what have been French Africa, British Africa, German or Italian, Belgian or Portuguese Africa.

Some of the African tribes are large enough to constitute homogenous and fairly populous national states, though none, except the Somalis, actually do. Most tribes are relatively small and merely aggravate the linguistic and national confusion in existing states. For instance, in certain parts of Nigeria it is possible to find, within a comparatively small area, half a dozen villages speaking not different

1 *New York Times Magazine,* April 20, 1958.

dialects but quite different languages. Further examples are provided by the Galla of Ethiopia, a minority dominated by the Amhara majority; by the Suku and Chaga of Tanganyika, the Kikuyu and Jur of Kenya, the Baganda and Ankole of Uganda; by the Hova, constituting a fourth of the population of Madagascar; and, besides, if we don't mind still longer cataloguing of unfamiliar tribal names, by the Mandingo, the Mossi, the Nupe, the Peuls, the Soughais, the Touareg, the Wolloff. Some such are contained in a single state; some overlap existing states.

Almost universally in Africa, and to some extent in Asia, there are two different and clashing types of what is currently described as nationalism. One is represented, say in Africa, by such contemporary Negro leaders as Kwame Nkrumah in Ghana, Sékou Touré in Guinea, Tom Mboyo in Kenya, Julius Nyerere in Tanganyika, and Mamadou Dea in Senegal. These and their colleagues have been educated in English or French schools. They not only aspire to "liberate" and transform former colonies into free national states modeled more or less after those in Europe, but also to repress native tribalism which they regard as an anachronistic survival of primitive barbarism and an obstacle to national unification and progress. They may welcome federation of existing states, as of Guinea with Ghana, or as the Mali union of Sudan with Senegal, but they want federation to be politically national rather than tribal.

On the other hand, tribalism is itself a type of nationalism, however primitive and on however small a scale.[1] In Africa it has had deep roots and long life, and modern attempts to suppress it, either by Europeans or by educated and progressive Negroes, have tended to give it added strength and resistance. For instance, the Mau Maus, who terrorized Kenya in the 1950's and sorely afflicted both British and fellow Negroes, were an oath-bound unit of Kikuyu, Meru, and Embu tribes; their nationalist movement has been crushed only after much bloodshed and the jailing of 60,000 tribesmen. Again, Negro tribesmen have vigorously and riotously opposed the incorporation of Nyasaland with white-ruled Northern and Southern

[1] See above, pp. 20–21.

Rhodesia in a "Central African Federation." Particularly significant is the contemporary warfare in the Belgian mandate of Ruanda. Here the conflict is not between blacks and whites, but between two tribes of blacks: (1) the tall, lordly Watusi, and (2) the shorter and historically servile Bahutu who fear lest in a future "freed" and national Ruanda they be again enslaved by the Watusi.

A news dispatch on the morrow of Christmas, 1959, tells of barbaric civil war in the heart of the Belgian Congo between Negro tribes of Lulua and Baluba. It "is being fought with primitive spears, bush knives, and arrows dipped in deadly poison. The Lulua are spurred on by naked women who brandish long wooden pot-stirrers. . . . The savagery of the fighting has upset even some militant nationalists, who are beginning to dread what might happen if the restraining influence of Belgian authority were suddenly lifted."[1] This proved too true. Tribal fighting and killing, and flight of frightened Europeans, followed promptly the relinquishment of Belgian authority in 1960.

It has been argued—I believe with far too much optimism—that the linguistic, and hence the tribal, problem in Africa will eventually be solved by spreading knowledge and use of some European language, say French or English, in the several emerging independent states. Certainly English or French, as a heritage of European imperialism, is familiar to the present leaders of these states and likewise, in greater or lesser degree, to other natives who have learned it in colonial or mission schools. But such persons are a very small segment of the total population. To render the great mass of African Negroes literate in English or French or any other European language would be a herculean task, and one which nationalists, intent upon freeing Africa from Europe, would hardly attempt.

In the extensive territories of Tanganyika and Kenya there may be a basis for national union of disparate tribes in the Swahili language which is a kind of *lingua franca* among them and which could become a common national language. And, of course, Arabic is a common literary language, as Islam is the common popular religion,

[1] Homer Bigart in *The New York Times*, Dec. 27, 1959.

in North Africa. Elsewhere, however, the multiplicity of tribes with different languages and customs—each, in a word, a distinctive nationality—militates against the unity of existing states and against any single-minded nationalism in them. The leaders must either subjugate the various tribes within national boundaries, as American Indian tribes were subjugated, and unite them in a common superior speech and loyalty, or else they must abandon hope of creating centralized nationalist states and content themselves with intertribal federations or empires. In either case, the way is likely to be long and arduous and bloody, and its outcome dubious. Indeed, tribal nationalism is as menacing as any foreign imperialism to the freedom and peace of Africa.

It is pertinent to add here that tribal organization and spirit, long divisive of Arab-speaking peoples, have latterly been lessened by an overspreading nationalism. This has been chiefly stimulated, we know, by common belligerent reaction against the supplanting of Arab Palestine by the nationalist Jewish state of Israel. It has already brought forward an Arab leader in the person of Gamal Abdel Nasser of Egypt and led to the combining of Syria with Egypt in a United Arab Republic. Other, if minor, disturbing nationalist threats to Asian peace include agitation among the Kurds of Turkey and Iraq for a free and united Kurdistan; the continuing desire for national unity of some sort on the part of Koreans, and also of Vietnamese; the strife between Pakistan and India over Kashmir, and the diverse languages and cultures within each; Tibetan and Indian nationalism against Chinese.

When we recall that it has taken a century and a half and a succession of deadly wars to redraw the political map of Europe along approximate lines of linguistic nationality, we may well wonder how long and what human holocausts it will take really to nationalize the far more extensive and complex continents of Asia and Africa?

CHAPTER XII

Reflections on the Religion
of Nationalism

1. The Cult[1]

Since its advent in western Europe, modern nationalism has partaken of the nature of a religion. This was exemplified, we have earlier noted, by such diverse apostles as Milton and Bolingbroke in England, by French Revolutionaries, by a "Vater" Jahn in Germany and a Mazzini in Italy. It is now evidenced throughout the world. Everywhere it has a god, who is either the patron or the personification of one's *patrie*, one's fatherland, one's national state. This deity may be referred to, in familiar, even jocular style as Uncle Sam, John Bull, Marianne, Hans, or Ivan. Yet it is the god of a chosen people, a jealous god, preeminently a god of battles.

Nationalism, like any religion, calls into play not simply the will, but the intellect, the imagination, and the emotions. The intellect constructs a speculative theology or mythology of nationalism. The imagination builds an unseen world around the eternal past and the everlasting future of one's nationality. The emotions arouse a joy and ecstasy in the contemplation of the national god who is all-good and all-protecting, a longing for his favors, a thankfulness for his benefits, a fear of offending him, and feelings of awe and reverence at the immensity of his power and wisdom; they express themselves naturally in worship, both private and public. For nationalism,

[1] This and the next section are taken in part from my *Essays on Nationalism,* ch. IV. Copyright, 1926, by The Macmillan Company.

again like any other religion, is social, and its chief rites are public rites performed in the name and for the salvation of a whole community.

Modern nationalism first arose among peoples that were traditionally Christian, and as a religion it has naturally borrowed and adapted to its own purposes many customs and usages of historic Christianity. To national State, as to universal Church, is attributable a mission of salvation and an ideal of immortality. The nation is conceived of as eternal, and the deaths of its loyal sons only add to its undying glory. It guards its members against any foreign devil, fosters for them the arts and sciences, and gives them nourishment. Nor may the role of national state be thought of as merely economic, much less mercenary. It is primarily spiritual, even other-worldly, and its driving force is its collective *faith*, a faith in its mission and destiny, a faith in things unseen, a faith that would move mountains.

There are certain striking parallels between contemporary nationalism and medieval Christianity. Nowadays the individual is born into the national state, and the secular registration of birth is the national rite of baptism. Thenceforth the state solicitously follows him through life, tutoring him in a national catechism, teaching him by pious schooling and precept the beauties of national holiness, fitting him for life of service (no matter how exalted or how menial) to the state, and commemorating his vital crises by formal registration (with a fee) not only of his birth but likewise of his marriage, of the birth of his children, and of his death. If he has been a crusader in behalf of nationalism, his place of entombment is marked with the ensign of his service. The funerals of national heroes and potentates are celebrated with magnificent pomp and circumstance, while, since World War I, a most sacred shrine in a nation's capital city is the "Tomb of the Unknown Soldier." Here shine perpetual lights. Here floral offerings ever repose.

Membership in some national state is compulsory. The individual may withdraw from the earthly State Militant only by death or emigration. The latter exit is now usually restricted, if not totally barred, and even if the individual can migrate, it is practically impossible for him to settle in any land which does not possess some established form of the religion of nationalism. He may change his sect, so to speak, but not the religion. And however skeptical one may be about the national faith, one knows that compulsory membership in any national state involves compulsory financial support of its maintenance and missionary enterprise, for such a state is more rigorously insistent upon the collection of taxes than any church ever was upon the levying of tithes.

Interior devotion to nationalism is expected of everybody, though in this respect a little allowance may appropriately be made for human frailty. So long as public rites and ceremonies are decently observed, the hearts of individual worshipers need not be too closely searched. Human beings doubtless differ in the intensity of their religious feelings, and some, perhaps, are so abnormal as not to experience any religious emotion. Besides, it has long been recognized that he who prays the loudest and beats his breast most ostentatiously may be sadly lacking in true interior devotion. The ways of skeptics and doubters have been notoriously subtle, and we may reasonably question whether Pharisees and whited sepulchers do not exist among the many sincerely devout nationalists.

There can be no question of the popular and compelling character of external nationalist worship. Blasphemy and sacrilege have customarily been regarded as heinous crimes, and the present-day person who allows a flitting mental doubt to find expression in sneer or jest at the expense of the national cult is eligible for madhouse or for jail.

The ritual of modern nationalism is simpler than that of certain other religions, but, considering its comparative youthfulness, it is already fairly well developed. Its chief symbol and central object of worship is the national flag. Strictly speaking, there was no such thing on the European Continent prior to the French Revolution of the late eighteenth century, and the stars and stripes of the United States are not much older. Now every nation in the world has a flag, and a good deal of ingenuity is required to invent distinctive arrangements of pattern and color for the eighty-odd members of the United Nations—and others yet to join.

There are universal liturgical forms for "saluting" the flag, for "dipping" the flag, for "lowering" the flag, and for "hoisting" the flag. Men bare their heads when the flag passes by; and in praise of the flag poets write odes, and to it children sing hymns and pledge allegiance. In all solemn feasts and fasts of nationalism, the flag is in evidence, and with it that other sacred thing, the national anthem. An acute literary critic in his purely secular capacity might be tempted to cavil at phrases in "Rule Britannia," in "Deutschland über Alles," or even in the "Marseillaise;" he might object, on literary grounds, to such a lame beginning as "Oh say, can you see?" But a national anthem is not a profane thing and does not admit of textual criticism. It is the *Te Deum* of the new dispensation; worshipers stand when it is intoned, the military at "attention" and the male civilians with uncovered heads, all with external show of respect and veneration.

Nationalism has its processions and pilgrimages. It has, too, its holy days, and just as the Christian Church adapted some festivals from Paganism, so the national state has borrowed from Christianity. In the United States, for example, the Fourth of July is a nationalist Christmas, Flag Day an adaptation of Corpus Christi, and Decoration Day or Veterans' Day a patriotic version of All Souls Day, while in imitation of the saints' days of the Christian calendar are observed the birthdays of national saints and heroes, such as Washington and Lincoln.

Nationalism likewise has its temples, and he who would find the places and structures that are held most sacred by the mass of Americans should seek not Christian cathedrals but Independence Hall in Philadelphia, Faneuil Hall in Boston, the Tomb of General Lee in Lexington and that of General Grant in New York, and, above all, the multidomed and columned national capital, a veritable mecca of popular pilgrimage, with its Temples of Congress and Supreme Court, its White House, its majestic monuments to Lincoln, Jefferson, and Washington, and its adjacent shrines of Arlington and Mount

Vernon. Among corresponding holy places in Europe, we might mention Westminster Abbey in London, the Arc de Triomphe in Paris, the Victor Emmanuel monument in Rome, the Kremlin in Moscow. And what similar shrines exist or impend in Delhi, Jakarta, and Cairo, in the capitals of Ghana, Sudan, and Congo!

Moderns may regard their medieval ancestors' veneration of images, icons, and relics as savoring of "superstition," but let them replace, say, a statue of St. Joseph with a graven image of Abraham Lincoln, an icon of the Blessed Virgin with a lithograph of Martha Washington or of the somewhat mythical Molly Pitcher, and a relic of the Holy Cross with a tattered battle flag, and they display a fitting reverence. If we recall the likenesses of national "fathers" and heroes which adorn both the sumptuous clubs of the wealthy and the simple cottages of the poor, we can appreciate the religious appeal of contemporary nationalism.

2. Mythology, Intolerance, and Sacrifice

From nationalist intellectuals come more or less lengthy and learned works on their countries' history and literature and character which are drawn upon and simplified by publicists and textbook authors. Then in due course the writings of these gentlemen (or ladies) are piously adapted and vulgarized, for popular consumption, by sentimental journalists and emoting orators. The outcome of the process is that a nationalist theology of intellectuals becomes a nationalist mythology for the masses.

This mythology is not in every detail strictly accurate and literally true (no mythology ever is), but after all its main purpose is didactic—"for example of life and instruction of manners," in the happy phrasing of Archbishop Cranmer; and didacticism need not slavishly depend, any more than poetry, upon historical or scientific fact. Take, for instance, a speech which a Congressman of mine delivered some years ago in the House of Representatives and which he relentlessly distributed, at government expense, among all his constituents. It is a nationalist homily and closes with a rousing paean:

"The military annals of mankind reveal no finer discipline, no more splendid heroism, than were displayed on every battlefield of the Revolution and the War between the States. The soldiers of Washington were no craven spirits, no mercenary hirelings imported from the shambles of Europe. . . . They were freemen, champions of human liberty. . . . No ignorant, vulgar rebels they! The Revolutionary ranks were filled with accomplished scholars, with men who read the tragedies of Aeschylus in Greek as easily as the tragedies of Shakespeare in English. Government, philosophy, and religion were themes of daily and familiar converse around colonial camp fires. The soldiers of the Revolution knew the richness of their blood. They traced their lineage along a noble line to Crécy, Poitiers, Malplaquet, and Ramillies. They read the military achievements of their race in the recovery of the holy sepulchre, in the battle at Hohenlinden, in the capture of Quebec. They felt no inability to multiply these brilliant deeds; and when the battle call was sounded by the bugle's stirring blast and the thrilling tones of the trumpet and the drum, it was then that the heroes of Saratoga and Yorktown, of Brandywine and Valley Forge, moved to the impetuous charge with the victors' exultant shout. It was then they stepped, 'like bridegrooms to a marriage feast,' into the jaws of death. . . .

"Mr. Speaker, I have an abiding and an unbounded faith in the great destiny and in the undying glory of my country. I believe that the time is not far distant when we shall have complete military and naval, economic and industrial, intellectual and spiritual preparedness; when American genius and American influence will dominate the nations and overshadow the earth; when our Constitution and our Declaration of Independence will be the mold and model of free institutions among all the tribes of men; when the torch of freedom which was lit at the flame of the American Revolution will be a beacon light to the oppressed of all mankind; when our soldiers and our sailors will be feared and respected on every land and on every sea; when the drumbeat of our country will be heard around the world; when freedom's flag will illumine all the skies; and, whether proceeding from the mouth of an ambassador or from the

hot throats of Federal guns, the mandate of the great Republic will
be heard and obeyed throughout the earth. (Applause.)"

Such a peroration doubtless sounded nobly dithyrambic to its
hearers, but it is more in the nature of myth or poetry than in that
of factual prose. The critical historian knows that there were battles
in the Revolutionary War and in the War between the States (for
instance, the First Battle of Bull Run) in which discipline and
heroism were not notably displayed. He also knows that the Revolutionary ranks were not exactly filled with men who read the tragedies
of Shakespeare (or anything else) in English, to say nothing of
reading Aeschylus in the original Greek.

Nor is it easy for a logically minded person, or one familiar with
current world-wide reaction against Western imperialism, to perceive
just how freedom's flag will illumine all the skies at the very time when
American soldiers and sailors are feared on every land and on every
sea. But these and other criticisms which might be leveled at the Congressman are beside the point.

The point is that the myths enshrined in the quotation have sprung
from a lively nationalist faith, and are justified on the ground that
they meet a national need so admirably that they must be true. They
are products of piety, and how can piety be immoral? How can edifi-
cation be false?

The school system of the national state is held to strict account for
any lapse from the official theology or for any slur upon the popular
mythology. If a bold teacher or a tactless textbook writer offers an
explanation of some episode in national history not in harmony with
the nationalist faith, he is liable to denunciation by some ultrapatriotic society or individual; he may be dismissed and the offensive text
banned and even burned.

For there is constant fear among heated patriots lest the masses
lose their nationalist faith, and determination, therefore, that only
such information should be imparted to them as will strengthen that
faith and promote popular devotion to it. As a "Committee on
Studies and Textbooks" of New York City declared in a famous report: "The textbook must contain no statement in derogation or in dis-

paragement of the founders of the Republic or of those who have guided its destinies; . . . the dominating spirit of the Revolution is found in the words of Nathan Hale: 'I regret that I have but one life to lose for my country.' "[1]

The religion of nationalism is apt to be intolerant of any sort of dissenters. Outright traitors are the worst: they are liable to quick death if they are caught, and in any case to the ignominy attached to the name of Benedict Arnold or Quisling or other "collaborationist." More numerous, and more difficult to deal with, are persons who are suspected of lacking in national loyalty or harboring a superior loyalty to another nation. Such unfortunates in times of great stress, especially during war—"cold" as well as "shooting"—are ferreted out with an ardor equaling that of a Torquemada, or a Cotton Mather on a witch hunt, and may be banished or jailed. Even in ordinary times, a watch must be kept for "crypto-heretics" who teach children or write for the masses. They are peculiarly dangerous, for they may be imperiling the nationalist souls of the little ones and the innocent.

Human beings do not normally and willingly give their lives for economic gain. The supreme sacrifice is oftenest paid for an ideal and in response to a religious sense; and the best and final proof of the religious character of modern nationalism is the unquestioning willingness with which all manner of its devotees have laid down their lives on battlefields of the last hundred and seventy years. All over northern France, for instance, there are hundreds of thousands of little whitewashed crosses bearing the same simple inscription, "Mort pour la patrie."

Modern nationalism has indeed been a peculiarly bloody religion. Vastly more persons have been slain in nationalist wars of the first half of the present century than in four centuries of medieval crusading. This is not merely because of new and greatly improved weapons. It is preeminently because the nationalist fighting of our time is totalitarian; it is mass, rather than class, warfare. And by the time the masses of Asia and Africa are rendered literate and duly in-

[1] *The Historical Outlook*, XIII, 255 (October, 1922).

doctrinated, and the whole world divided among linguistically based national states, what numberless wars may have been waged and what gigantic human holocausts may have been sacrificed.

Nationalism of the present age has an ever growing number of jealous and quarrelsome sects. It is also, as a whole, the latest and nearest approach to a world religion. Its cult is now universal, and is accompanied as well by African tom-tom as by European or American fife and drum.

3. Moderating Influences

The dark prospect of world-wide nationalist fanaticism and an unending series of nationalist wars is at least partially lightened by the presence of contrary tendencies and moderating influences. One is a new spurt of pacifism, resulting from popular realization that war can hardly be localized any more and that another World War, waged with all the bombs and missiles which the latest science and technology could produce, would be too awful, too catastrophic, to contemplate or to endure. Statesmen of the Soviet Union and the United States vie with each other in making world tours on professed peace missions, and in clamoring for disarmament and a ban on the new weapons.

One can be overly optimistic about such pacifism. Contemporary statesmen are not the first to advocate disarmament, and probably, in view of the nationalism of themselves and their respective peoples, they will not be the first to achieve it. Finances may compel its reduction, but not abstract pacifism or humanitarian sentiment. Novel weapons of offense are always alarming at first, but the alarm usually leads to the invention of new weapons of defense and on to an actual increase of competitive armaments. Every national state has a high-ranking cabinet "Minister of War," or, more euphemistically, "Secretary of Defense"; none that I know of has a Secretary or Minister of Peace.

Another World War would indeed be dreadful, and it would be so because it would result, not only in enormous destruction of life and goods, but most probably also, like its predecessors, in an access of national hatreds and international injustice. A national state, particularly a democratic national state, is apt to devote itself so exclusively to fighting and winning a war as to incapacitate it for concluding a sane and lasting peace. The United States, for example, while playing a decisively victorious part in both World Wars I and II, must bear a large measure of responsibility for losing the peace after each. After the first, it withdrew into itself, stubbornly repudiating international cooperation with the League of Nations, blindly insisting on collecting war debts from its former Allies, stupidly banishing the teaching of German in its public schools, and indirectly undermining the German Republic and paving the way for Hitler. During and immediately after the Second World War, such slogans as "unconditional surrender," such a short-sighted project as that of Secretary Morgenthau's for converting industrialized Germany into a peasant country, and such theatrical public shows as the Nuremberg Trials, evidenced national hatred of the current enemy but no appreciation that there might be in the future another and more menacing enemy against whom the aid of a strong and democratic Germany might be wanted.

To be sure, the United States, since World War II, has reversed the stand it took after World War I against international organization, and, along with all other national states of the world, is now a member—a very active member—of the United Nations. This organization may not prevent war: it has not done so in Korea or Vietnam. But it performs valuable cooperative service in manifold ways, and, most significant, it testifies to a growing conviction that nationalism must be tempered by internationalism. Of course the thinking of statesmen and the schooling of the masses remain much more national than international, and in any vital conflict between the two during the foreseeable future the national is most likely to prevail. Nationalism has that popular "religious" appeal which internationalism as yet lacks.

Whether or not in the long run all the many nations of the world, including liberal democratic, communist or other dictatorial, and primitively tribal, can compose their respective nationalisms and act together peacefully as "United Nations," is highly problematical. On a smaller scale, however, there are now several notable examples of national *federations* in which each member puts restraint on its own nationalism and even yields some degree of its sovereignty for the sake of what it regards as a larger common good. Thus, to forward the supposed common good of communism, the nations of the Soviet Union and its satellite nations act on crucial matters as a unit; and if the whole world turned Communist, there might be, as Marx and Lenin predicted, a world of peace—and also, as others believe, a world of slavery and despotism.

On the other hand, federations have been formed for defense of the "free world" against Communist aggression: NATO (North Atlantic Treaty Organization), with fifteen members and a permanent headquarters staff at Paris; SEATO (South East Asia Treaty Organization), with eight members; METO (Middle East Treaty Organization), with five members. Moreover, for mutual aid in economic development, there is the so-called "Colombo" plan, operated by a federal organization of eighteen nations of southern and southeastern Asia. Especially noteworthy is the federation of six nations of Western Europe (France, Belgium, the Netherlands, Luxembourg, Italy, and West Germany) in an economic community, the "European Common Market," with internal free trade and pooling of resources. And about this central group of six, an "outer" and looser group of seven other West European nations (Great Britain, Norway, Sweden, Denmark, Switzerland, Austria, and Portugal) are now pursuing common trade policies. All this, despite difference of language and centrifugal force of nationalism, may portend the advent, in time, of a substantial United States of Western Europe.

We should note likewise such institutions as the British Commonwealth, the Pan-American Organization of twenty-one nations in the "New World," and the French Community of Nations. These may be more honorific than effective, and none of them proof against nationalist disruption. Yet they do embody an *ideal* of international cooperation and friendship beyond and above the isolations and enmities fostered by extreme and exclusive nationalism. Nowadays, too, better and faster means of communication have greatly expedited travel and trade between nations and correspondingly made available more information about one another than ever before.[1] Wherein is a chance of increasing nationalist feeling and friction, but also a good chance of promoting mutual understanding.

Perhaps in Asia and Africa, where nationalism is a comparatively recent development, it can be moderated and rendered less provocative of war through adoption and application of the principles of federation and democracy. These have secured peace and united action among three nationalities in Switzerland (German, French, Italian) and between two in Canada (British and French). They may conceivably do the same in polyglot India, and eventually among the hodgepodge of tribes in the Congo, the Sudan, or Rhodesia, in East or West Africa. At the moment, this savors of wishful thinking. The problem of language, and its intimate relationship with national or tribal tradition and entity, remains a very big and real problem for anyone who imagines that nationalism has reached its zenith.

Liberal democracy, as we have elsewhere said, is quite compatible with nationalism. Both are phases of the acquisition of political power by the masses. But nationalism under democratic rule has proved itself during the last half-century in Europe and America less virulent, less belligerent than under dictatorship, and less disturbing to world peace. Under a dictatorship, such as Napoleon's or Hitler's or Stalin's, decisions for aggression and war, as for everything, can be made quickly in accordance with the dictator's personal ambition and will, and patriotic mass support assured by dictatorial propaganda and duress. A democracy is more cumbersome, more sluggish in action. Its government usually follows, rather than creates, public opinion, and has qualms about abridging personal liberties and censoring press criticism. In a word, war, the ultimate in nationalism, is a more arduous undertaking for democracy than for dictatorship. And it is to be hoped—though perhaps against hope—that

---

[1] Exception has to be made for peoples shut off by "iron" or "bamboo" curtains.

emergent national states in Asia and Africa will prefer the democratic and liberal type of nationalism to the dictatorial and totalitarian. The latter, we must confess, is likely to have greater appeal, and to work less troublesomely, for nationalists who are in a hurry.

Art and science and technology are not the possession of any one nation. They have always spread from one to another, and now faster than ever. They are utilized, we well know, for nationalist purposes, but at the same time they provide bridges between nationalities. In fact, they can be, to change the metaphor, quiet undercover agents of internationalism, a kind of unobserved termite.

There are, moreover, the great historic cultural areas which overlap national boundaries and exert an international influence. Western Europe has had for centuries, and still retains, a distinctive civilization with *mores* and art-forms to which nations within its orbit are co-heirs and hence sharers in certain common traditions that transcend nationalism. The same can be said of the Far East, of the subcontinent of India, of the Middle and Near East. True, these cultural areas are now losing a considerable part of their former distinctiveness. On the one hand, they are being caught up and brought together by the overspreading of a common material civilization; on the other, they are being torn apart by nationalism. What, then, becomes of the supernatural world religions—Christianity, Islam, Hinduism, Buddhism—which are the spiritual bases of the several cultural areas just mentioned and which have been great historic factors in internationalism and cosmopolitanism?

4. Interaction of Nationalism and Historic World Religions, Especially Christianity

Modern and contemporary nationalism, I repeat, appeals to man's "religious sense." It offers a substitute for, or supplement to, historic supernatural religion. Persons indifferent or hostile to the latter are apt to find a compensatory satisfaction and devotion in this-worldly nationalism, that is, in what is essentially a religion of modern secularism. Which incidentally explains how people can be at once Communist and nationalist.

Nationalism, being also a very sectarian religion, tends to be intolerant of any possible rival religion. In combination with materialistic and dictatorial communism, it opposes and persecutes Christianity and Judaism, as in the Soviet Empire; "red" China not only kills, jails, or expels Christian missionaries but subjugates the Buddhist Tibetans and drives their Dalai Lama into exile. Elsewhere, in non-Communist countries, the national state is commonly deemed superior in authority to any church, and persons who are suspected of acting or thinking otherwise are likely to be charged with "divided allegiance" and regarded at best as second-class citizens.

The religion of nationalism, as we pointed out at the beginning of this chapter, has borrowed for its cult from older world religions, especially the Christian. In turn, the older religions show a tendency to accept and even forward nationalism. Thus develops a religious syncretism, or admixture, by virtue of which multitudes of people throughout the world continue at least nominally to adhere to the faith of their ancestors and to practice its cult while they adapt it to the exigencies of nationalist worship and discipline.

Supernatural historic Judaism remains a potent force in the lives of many Jews, but a large number of them now express their "religious sense" in a "higher" nationalism, either that of the people among whom they live or that of Zionism and the new national state of Israel. Buddhism is still an important factor in the lives of myriad Orientals, but it has latterly been subordinated in Japan to nationalist Shinto, in China to communism, and in Burma and Ceylon to emergent national states. Islam, too, is still a great and proselyting religion, with far-flung missionary enterprise in the East Indies and in Africa, but the followers of Mustafa Kemal and Riza Shah Pahlavi have proved themselves Turkish or Iranian nationalists first and Muslims afterward, and Muslim Arabs fraternize with Christian Arabs in common devotion to Arab nationalism against Jewish nationalism.

Christianity has more nominal followers today than ever before, and probably more devout disciples—Catholic, Orthodox, and Protestant. But for many it is actually an adjunct to nationalism. Westminster Abbey is a fane of the Church of England and, more so, of British nationalism; and Protestant cathedrals of England and Scotland, of New York and Washington, are adorned not so plentifully or so conspicuously with statues of Christian saints as with images and memorials of national heroes, military and naval, and with national battle flags. In France the remains of Napoleon Bonaparte are enshrined beside a Catholic altar, and the once magnificent Christian church of Sainte Geneviève has been transformed into a national Pantheon. In Spanish churches the silence that normally attends the consecration and elevation of the Host is broken at high mass by loud organ rendition of the national anthem.

Syncretism of nationalism and Christianity is strikingly noticeable in the United States. Here it is abetted by the religio-cultural pluralism of a Protestant majority, distributed among a hundred or more churches and sects, a large Catholic minority of varied ethnic background, and a smaller but very active Jewish minority. Each of such groups appears bent on outdoing the others in ostentatious devotion to American ideals and institutions. In most Protestant churches a big American flag hangs resplendent over the pulpit or communion table, and national holidays are ceremoniously observed. Catholic churches and Jewish synagogues display rosters of members who have fought and died for the nation. "Fundamentalists" deduce from their literal Biblical faith an inspiring parallel between the "chosen" Hebrew people of antiquity and the "chosen" American people of modern times. Religious "modernists" and "liberals" seem to thicken Americanism in measure as they dilute Christianity.

We recall, for example, the illuminating report of a service held after World War I at the Protestant Episcopal Church of St. Mark's-in-the-Bouwerie, in New York City. Along with a sermon in which a clergyman of the Modern Churchman's Union "denied the divinity of Christ," ritual worship of the American flag "engaged the attention of large congregations morning and afternoon."

"The worship," the report goes on to say, "was performed on a platform in front of the chancel by professional actors as Chief Officiant, the Son; First Assistant, the Mother; and Second Assistant, the

Father. . . . the seven impersonators of the red stripes in the flag were named as Washington, Jefferson, Jackson, Lincoln, Cleveland, [T.] Roosevelt, and Wilson. [How unfortunate for F.D.R. and Ike that the stripes don't number nine!]

"The white flagstaff was placed in front of the sanctuary and topped with a golden sphere over which hovered the golden eagle. The congregation was addressed. . . . 'The eagle is the emblem of our sovereignty; he expresses our aspiration and our inspiration, our living communion with the God of our fathers.' This was followed by the psalm of the eagle. After the psalm the Chief Officiant cried aloud: 'Hear ye the cry of the eagle.' The congregation responded: 'Let us rally to obey.' The flag was then raised to the singing of the first stanza of the Star-Spangled Banner, while the Chief Officiant said: 'Let us raise a standard to which the wise and the honest can repair.'

"In the second part of the ritual the congregation were bidden to lift up their eyes to the seven red stripes, 'as they are well worthy of worship.' This chorus followed:

" 'To the red of the flag
" 'The red of the flag, the red of the flag,
" 'To the red of the flag forever.'

In like manner was performed the ritual of the six white stripes, the square of the midnight blue, the five-pointed white stars. The final ceremony was the worship of the white-hooded eagle. At the conclusion the flag was allowed to drop on the flagstaff as a salute to the sanctuary [gracious concession!], and the Battle Hymn of the Republic was sung."[1]

To some readers the account of nationalism presented in the foregoing pages will doubtless seem too pessimistic, too adversely critical. True, nationalism is only one form—a modern and contemporary form—of exalting and deifying the secular state. An ancient city-state like Sparta or empire like the Assyrian or Alexander the Great's or Diocletian's (or the medieval Mongol) was hardly less warlike and intolerant, and hardly less demanding of supreme religious

[1] *The New York Times,* Feb. 25, 1924.

worship, than the modern state based on nationality. The difference is primarily one of degree. Industrial and technological progress has made available to the contemporary national state means of training and indoctrinating its citizens which earlier empires and city-states lacked. Thereby nationalism is enabled to become a resuscitated, large-scale tribalism, accompanied by a religion of nationalism widely popular and deeply devout.

We can perceive, nevertheless, certain utility and advantage in nationalism as it has arisen and spread in modern times. In Europe and America, that is throughout Christendom, it has been a stimulus to internal reform and betterment within the several countries progressively affected by it. It has fostered literacy and schooling for the masses, made them members of the body politic, and given them a sense of the responsibilities, as well as of the rights, of citizenship. It has usually been a phase of the democratic spirit and apparently compatible, in most of the Western world, with a large amount of individual liberty and likewise with internationalism and humanitarianism. Over against dictatorial and totalitarian nationalists—say Stalin, Mussolini, or Hitler—should be set such liberal and humanitarian nationalists as Herder and Mazzini, Woodrow Wilson and Winston Churchill, Konrad Adenauer and Charles de Gaulle. And many another!

We have remarked a contemporary tendency to adapt, if not to subordinate, Christianity to nationalism and have cited an extreme example of it in connection with a "ritual worship" of the American flag in a New York church. But this is only one side of the story. For it must be stressed, on the other side, that, despite external attacks and internal subversion, Christianity remains with multitudes a live and effective religion and that its creed and moral teachings exert a most important moderating influence on nationalism.

Indeed, nationalism seems to owe its better features in large part to Christianity. The Christian Church has long regarded patriotism as a needful and ennobling virtue; and ecclesiastical organization and functioning along lines of nationality antedated and contributed to the rise of national states. But at the same time it set bounds to excessive nationalism by its insistent claim to be catholic, that is, universal, for all men and all nations, and also by its persistent teaching of the precept of its Founder that, while Christians were to render to Caesar what is his, they were to render to God what is His. In other words the demands of earthly nationalism must not be confused, for the Christian, with those of supernatural religion; he does indeed have a divided allegiance, for above and beyond his national loyalty is his duty of loyalty to Christian faith and morals.[1]

Christian faith and morals may differ in detail, depending on whether they are interpreted by Catholic pope and bishops, by Orthodox Church councils, or by Protestant reading of the Scriptures. There is, nevertheless, a common Christian heritage; and now, when Christianity as a whole is sorely beset and critically threatened, not only by materialistic communism, but by aggressive and antagonistic nationalism, there is an obvious ecumenical trend among leaders of its major divisions toward greater mutual charity and understanding. Certainly it is uniform Christian teaching that all nations, like all individuals, are, or should be, subject to a common international morality according to which each nation, instead of being an end in itself, would be a means to the well-being of all. Against potential pride and selfishness of unlimited nationalism, Christianity holds up ideals of humility and altruism.

To be effective, however, in leavening nationalism and limiting its excesses, professed Christians need to take their religion seriously and to seek to maintain it as a truly world religion superior to divisive nationalist religion. They cannot allow their own natural patriotism to become imbued with racialism or jingoism or other mark of the worst kind of narrow nationalism.

At present, as nationalism runs like a forest fire all over Asia and Africa, we have reason to wonder whether it will turn out to be destructive of historic world religions or whether it will be moderated and watered down by them. I lack the knowledge, and still less the

---

[1] I have dealt specifically and at some length with these points in "The Church and Nationalism," *Catholic Historical Review*, XXVIII, 1–12 (1942), and in *Patriotism, Nationalism and the Brotherhood of Man*, brochure No. 25 of Catholic Association for International Peace (1937).

foresight, to hazard a guess about the impact and influence of such religions on the future course of nationalism in areas historically Hindu or Confucian or Buddhist or Muslim. As a Christian, I earnestly believe that in measure as lands of Africa and Asia tolerate Christian missions (that are themselves without taint of European imperialism), and come under the influence of Christian faith and morals, the rising obsessive nationalism on those continents will be rendered less exclusive and belligerent and more in keeping with international cooperation and peace. And who, after two World Wars, doesn't want peace?

Index of Persons

A
Aaron, 11
Aasen, Ivar, 69
Acomb, Evelyn M., 103
Adenauer, Konrad, 3, 180
Aeschylus, 169, 170
Agricola, Julius, 40
Alba, Duke of, 37
Alexander the Great, 22, 26, 143, 146
Alexander I, Tsar, 64
Alexander III, Tsar, 94, 108, 111
Alfieri, Vittorio, 46, 62–63
Angell, Norman, 122
Ariosto, 31
Aristotle, 143
Arndt, Ernst, 62
Arnold, Benedict, 171
Atatürk, 1, 131. See Kemal, Mustafa
Augustine, Saint, 90

B
Balfour, Arthur J., 124, 133
Barère, Bertrand, 50
Barzun, Jacques, 106
Beale, Georgia Robison, 50
Beethoven, 68
Ben-Gurion, David, 160
Bentham, Jeremy, 71
Bernadotte, Marshal, 60
Bernhardi, Friedrich von, 91
Bernstein, Eduard, 16
Bigart, Homer, 162
Bismarck, Otto von, 75, 78–79, 83, 85, 95, 103, 110, 120
Boccaccio, 31
Bolingbroke, Lord, 42, 44, 45, 164
Bolívar, Simón, 63
Bonald, Vicomte de, 60, 61
Bonaparte, Napoleon. See Napoleon Bonaparte

Boulanger, General, 108
Bright, John, 94
Brisson, Henri, 104
Brissot, de Warville, J. P., 46
Brutus, 46
Bryce, Lord, 21
Buddha, Gautama, 11, 24
Bülow, Bernhard von, 91–92
Burke, Edmund, 60, 61
Burns, Robert, 48
Buthman, W. C., 137

C
Caesar, Julius, 20, 143
Camoëns, Luis de, 32
Camus, Armand, 54
Cardwell, Lord, 80
Carnot, Lazare, 50, 58
Carroll, Charles, 49
Carroll, John, 49
Castro, Fidel, 153
Cavour, Count, 69, 74, 120
Cervantes, 32
Chaconas, Stephen C., 63
Chamberlain, Houston Stewart, 108, 140
Charles I, Austrian Emperor, 125
Charles II, of England, 40
Chateaubriand, Vicomte de, 61
Chaucer, 32, 39
Chaumette, P. G., 46
Chénier, M.-J. de, 55
Chiang Kai-shek, 134–135, 147, 153
Chopin, Frédéric, 68
Christ, Jesus, 11, 24, 26, 181
Churchill, Sir Winston, 149, 180
Clemenceau, Georges, 104
Cleveland, Grover, 179
Clough, Shepard B., 66

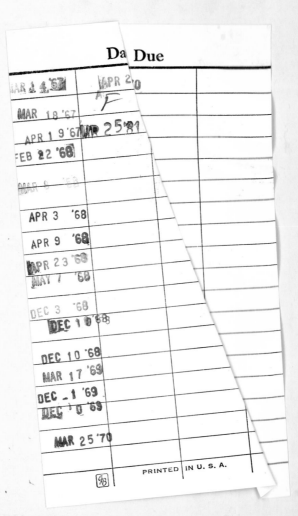

Da Due

MAR 14 '67	APR 2 0	
MAR 18 '67		
APR 1 9 '67	APR 25 81	
FEB 22 '68		
MAR 9 '68		
APR 3 '68		
APR 9 '68		
APR 23 '68		
MAY 7 '68		
DEC 3 '68		
DEC 1 0 '68		
DEC 10 '68		
MAR 17 '69		
DEC 1 '69		
DEC 1 0 '69		
MAR 25 '70		

PRINTED IN U. S. A.